The Real Man Inside:

This extremely well-written and remarkably personal book offers a sympathetic but deep and thoroughly balanced understanding of the men's movement. It additionally performs a particularly valuable service by forcefully demonstrating to those Christians who are deeply suspicious of the New Age movement that the "movement of men," rather than subverting Christian doctrine, is, at its core, utterly and wholesomely in accord with the gospels and both the teachings and the personhood of Jesus. I heartily recommend this as the best book I know on the subject.

—*M. Scott Peck*

Other books by Verne Becker:

Love Broke Through
   with Thomas B. Stribling

Tough Parenting for Dangerous Times
   with Andy Bustanoby

What They Never Told Me When I Became a Christian
   with Philip Yancey and Tim Stafford

The Campus Life Guide to Surviving High School
   (editor)

Safe Sex

The Real Man Inside

*How Men Can Recover Their Identity
and Why Women Can't Help*

VERNE BECKER

ZondervanPublishingHouse
Grand Rapids, Michigan
A Division of HarperCollins*Publishers*

Requests for information should be addressed to:
Zondervan Publishing House
Grand Rapids, Michigan 49530

Library of Congress Cataloging-in-Publication Data

Becker, Verne.
      The real man inside : how men can recover their identity and why
women can't help / Verne Becker.
            p.   cm.
      Includes bibliographical references.
      ISBN 0-310-54990-6 (hardcover)
      1. Men—United States—Psycholoty. 2. Identity (Psycholoty)—
United States. 3. Passivity (Psychology)—United States. 4. Masculinity
(Psychology)—United States. I. Title.
      HQ1090.3B43   1992
      155.3'32—dc20   92-12207
                                                                          CIP

Printed in the United States of America

92 93 94 95 96 / DH / 10 9 8 7 6 5 4 3 2 1

This edition is printed on acid-free paper and meets the American
National Standards Institute Z39.48 standard.

To my father

Contents

Acknowledgments

I wish to thank the following people for their input—conscious or unconscious—in the writing of this book:

The many poets, storytellers, and musicians who have served to awaken deeper parts of me that cannot be reached by logic, intellect, or propositional thinking.

Robert Bly, Sam Keen, John A. Sanford, Robert Moore and Douglas Gillette, M. Scott Peck, Robert A. Johnson, Rainer Maria Rilke, and others whose writings have influenced and challenged me.

The English department at Wheaton College, Illinois, especially the late professor Joe McClatchey, who first gave me a glimpse of the power of myth, and Paul Fromer, who encouraged my growth as a writer. Thanks also to Marjorie Mead at the Wade Center for her assistance in the area of myth.

The men of the Monday Night Men's Support Group of Glen Rock, New Jersey, who have been an integral part of my own journey away from passivity and toward wholeness, who remind me every week that I have a long way to go on this journey, and who encourage me to stay on that path. Thanks also to those who allowed their stories to be told (anonymously) at several points in this book.

Earl Laman, my therapist, mentor, and friend, who has helped me more than any other human being to explore my inner self and live more consciously and actively. Were it not for the incredible growth I have experienced through our personal and professional relationship, I would never have even known my male identity was missing, much less bothered to look for it.

Harold Myra and Barrie Peterson for reading the manuscript and offering valuable suggestions.

Bob Hudson at Zondervan for his enthusiasm and skillful editing on this project, as well as for his friendship.

Finally, I want to thank my wife, Nancy, who not only encouraged me early in our marriage to listen to my deeper self, but who also challenged me later on to write about what I was hearing. I am deeply grateful for her love and support, not only in the writing of this book but in the awakening of my truer self.

Introduction

It starts with an unsettling rattle.[1] Something makes you stop and ask: What's going on with my life? You have the basic trappings of a good life—wife, house, car. Or else you've had these things but have recently lost them. In either case, you know you're not really happy. The fact is, you don't really know what you feel or even who you are. Sure, you're aware of the roles people say you're supposed to fill, and you do a pretty good job of filling them. But deep inside, you feel numb, hypnotic, robotic, as if your soul had gone to sleep and your body was on autopilot.

Often the rattle occurs during your thirties. Sometimes it coincides with a crisis or loss in your life—an accident, an illness, unemployment, death, divorce.

Hearing the rattle at these times can be frightening. Shortly after I reached my thirties, I realized I heard a rattle too—a rattle of unhappiness and dissatisfaction. I hadn't done anything particularly awful in my life; but somehow I sensed I'd been sleepwalking for many years, and the alarm was now buzzing.

I first heard its sound when my wife announced that she was leaving me.

During that time of turmoil, separation, and divorce, I tried to listen to the rattle. I prayed. I went to a therapist. I racked my brain for something I could have done to make my wife want to leave me. I had never been physically or emotionally abusive. I had a steady job. I was warm and affectionate. I shared in the raising of our son. I was an excellent listener. I encouraged her to pursue her interests—either at home or in the workplace. I got along with her family. I was a nice guy. I did all the things society says that I, as a man, should do. So in the absence of any crimes on my part I concluded that the whole thing must have been her problem, and I tried to move on with my life.

Not long after my divorce I met Nancy, a former hippie with red hair, freckles, hazel Irish eyes, and a deep soul. She had gone through a lot of pain in her life, most recently the death of her father. At one level we saw in each other a resolution to the pain we had each experienced, though we knew that our relationship could never really resolve such pain; but at a deeper level, we were truly growing into a solid love for each other. When we married eight months later, we knew we had both made a fundamentally healthy choice for our lives.

Not long into my new marriage, however, the rattle, which had quieted for a while, returned. Now I was even more confused: My problem the first time around, I thought, was that I had married the wrong person. So I had assumed that by marrying the right person—Nancy—the rattle would stop. But it didn't.

I decided to pay closer attention to this rattle. I lifted my head, cocked my ear toward the sound, and tried to search out its source with my eyes, much as I scan the trees in my backyard when I hear the tapping of a woodpecker. I continued my therapy, exploring my childhood relationships with my mother and father, and identifying unhealthy aspects of my upbringing that I had carried into my marriage.

I also came into contact with other men whose wives had walked out on them. The stories they told were startlingly similar to mine: nice Christian guys, faithful to their wives and families, respected in their churches and communities, until one day their wives had called it quits. Even among my own friends I noticed it. Three of my close buddies from

Wheaton College in Illinois got married at about the same time I did, but within five years all three marriages had dissolved—all at the wives' initiative. My marriage had lasted the longest, but it had ended just like the others.

I began to wonder if a pattern was emerging. My first thought, as before, was to blame the women. After all, they were the ones who had chosen to leave. No doubt they had plenty of their own problems and issues to deal with. But the more I reflected on it, the more I began to see disturbing similarities among the men of these marriages, including myself. We all tended to let life happen to us, rather than pursuing the kind of life we really wanted. We reacted a lot more than we acted. When tough issues needed to be faced, we usually waited for our wives to address them, and then we tended to let them blow over (temporarily) rather than tackle and solve them. We helped with the kids or with household chores, but usually we had to be asked. Our friendships, our church involvement, even our family activities seemed to be carried on out of obligation rather than conviction. Our faith survived mostly in terms of beliefs that we assented to, but we felt little or no personal connection with God. We also felt somewhat confused about what our roles were. Though most of us pursued careers, none of us had a clear sense of what we wanted out of life, and few of us did much to find out. There was a kind of monotony to life, at least to our inner life.

In short, we lived empty, passive lives. We had little sense of our identity as men. We could be nice, we could be helpful, we could even be sensitive; but we didn't know how to be real, how to seize the day and live out of our deepest desire. So how could we offer much of our selves to our wives? We didn't even know who our selves were. Certainly our ex-wives too must be accountable for their actions and their choices, but if we husbands had developed a clearer, crisper sense of our identities, perhaps fewer of these marriages would have ended.

Just as I began to arrive at some of these realizations, I became aware of a growing phenomenon across the country often called the "men's movement," popularized by the poet Robert Bly. It happened quite by "accident" one day in early 1990 as I scanned the TV channels with the remote control. I landed on the PBS special *A Gathering of Men,* in which Bill Moyers interviews Bly. The poet spoke of the emptiness and confusion men have felt about their identities, and of the alienation the past few generations of men have felt from their fathers, and therefore from themselves.

As I sat on the couch, riveted to that interview, I realized that Bly was touching on the exact issues I—along with millions of other men—was dealing with after my first marriage ended. I even heard the rattle again. But after hearing Bly, I didn't lift up my head as before and scan the treetops for the source of the sound. Instead, I lowered my head until my chin touched my chest, and I focused my gaze on my own heart, and, just behind it, my soul. Now I knew: The rattle was coming from within me, from within my own soul. And at that moment I realized that if I was to reawaken my soul and find my identity, my true self as God created me, I would have to go down, down into myself.

I mentioned the show to my brother-in-law, John. He had seen it and been similarly affected. So had several of his friends. Before long a number of us got together to view a videotape of the show and discuss it, and a men's support group had begun. The Monday Night Men's Support Group has met in an Episcopal church in Glen Rock, New Jersey, every week for more than two years. Ten to twenty men attend each meeting, and I have learned that men's groups similar to this one are forming all over the country. Surprisingly, the men don't sit around and complain about their wives or girlfriends. Instead, we want to take responsibility for our lives. We are sick of being passive and out of touch with ourselves and God. We get together in order to grieve over the wounds we received and the choices we made that have led us to be passive men. We talk about our past and present experiences as we attempt to reclaim our lost identities. And we express our desire to enjoy healthy, rich, meaningful relationships with women, with each other, with our children, and with God. It's one way of going down, a way of listening to and honoring the rattle within rather than thumping it into silence as we do the morning alarm.

Going down into oneself is a difficult, fearful, ongoing process. Once we begin, we realize that we have lost many things, and we must grieve over their loss. In many ways, this is a book about loss, many different kinds of loss. About the loss of a father, the loss of a childhood many of us never had, the loss of life-passion, the loss of identity, the loss of meaning, the loss of a marriage or of the spark in a marriage, the loss of richness and depth in our relationship to God.

But it is also a book about recovering some of those things. That is what many people mean when they say they are "in recovery"—they have lost something and they're trying to find it again, to recover it. For me, and for those men reading this book, what we are trying to recover is our very identity.

"The purposes of a man's heart are deep waters," says the book of Proverbs, "but a man of understanding draws them out." When we take the time and effort to go down, down beneath the rocky, stony shells of men that we are, we will find water: Deep water, flowing water, living water, soul-water that quenches the deepest thirst, gives birth to new life, and wells up from within to overflow into the world around us.

Western society is jammed with men who, like us, are struggling with issues of identity. In this book I've used the term *passive* to describe these men. They may be single, married, or formerly married, but they're beginning to realize that life is passing them by. If their wives or girlfriends have not actually left, they're probably complaining that they don't get enough of what they need. And what is it that women really want from their men? I believe that ultimately it is not more love or sex or money or freedom. They need a man who knows, loves, and accepts himself fully, and who actively, consciously, brings this whole person into all aspects of his life, including his relationships with women. Most women want neither John Wayne nor Pee Wee Herman. They want a man who knows how to be real, a man who can take responsibility for himself, and a man who can take responsibility within a relationship.

But my point is not that men should learn to give women what they need. Yes, they should, but first they must learn to feel and meet their own needs. They need to grapple with the basic questions of life such as Who am I? What are my innermost needs, hurts, desires, and motivations? What gives me the greatest joy, the deepest satisfaction? What is worth living for—really living for? What is my highest calling? A man who doesn't know himself can never truly give of himself. All he can do is play a role, meet an obligation, fulfill his duty, and in so doing stamp out the tiny flame of his true self, the purposeful, passionate, real man inside.

Discovering that inner man, first because he is infinitely worth finding, and second because he is worth giving to others, is what this book is about. While this is a book about men, and primarily for men, I believe women can also benefit from it. Perhaps couples could even read and discuss it together. I would guess that many of the stages in a man's search for identity have parallels for women. But the man's journey is unique, as is a woman's, and I have chosen to explore the masculine side. If indeed there are millions of passive men out there, however, then there are also millions of frustrated, angry women. Maybe this book will help those women develop greater understanding, and possibly more patience, for the struggling men in their lives. It might even help women by relieving them of unrealistic pressures to meet all of a man's emotional needs. But it is important for both women and men to realize that a man must find his identity on his own. Thus the book's subtitle, "—Why Women Can't Help." A woman can certainly help by loving and supporting and dialoguing with her partner, but she can't change him. Only he can do that, if and when he is ready. I sincerely hope that for those men who are ready, this book may contribute to the process.

One

The Passive Man

*Women want mediocre men, and men are working
hard to become as mediocre as possible.*

—*Margaret Mead*

Picture a lazy bum who does nothing but lie around watching ballgames on TV and drinking beer. Or the nerdy wimp George McFly, father of Michael J. Fox's character, Marty, in *Back to the Future*. Call these guys passive men, and everyone understands. But there are millions of men in today's world who are nothing like these two stereotypes, who work hard at their jobs, love their wives or girlfriends, provide for their families, and yet still qualify as passive men. They may not know it, but they have adopted a passive approach to life, regardless of their profession, economic status, ethnic or religious ties. Salesmen, advertising executives, doctors, soldiers, policemen, assembly-line workers, ministers, builders, entrepreneurs, artists, and athletes can all be passive men. And their passivity is causing problems with their spouses or girlfriends, bosses, coworkers, but mostly within themselves.

I know this because I myself am a passive man. For years I have cruised through life without knowing who I really am. Right now I would call myself a passive man who is trying to change; and in order to change I'm in the process of owning up to a lot of things about myself. As I've shared what I'm like with other men, many have said, "Yeah—I'm like that too." And a few women have responded, "Gee, that sounds a lot like my husband [or boyfriend]." So in this chapter I'll attempt to paint a picture of passive men, their approach to life, and why we need to change.

Passive Men Are Nice Guys

Sometimes they're too nice for their own good. I don't consider myself a bad or a difficult person. In fact, I'm friendly and find it easy to relate to people in a casual way. Introduce me to someone, and I'm likely to ask them about their family, their work, and their interests, and they'll go away saying, "You know, Verne sure is a friendly guy, isn't he?" I tend to respect men and women equally, though I may give women a little more attention. I have a good sense of humor. I can make people laugh. I know how to kid around with people. Publicly, I tend to look on the bright side. I'm generally up.

My niceness comes largely out of a desire to please other people. I want to be liked. In a group, I won't give anyone trouble if I hear something I disagree with or even something that offends me; I tend to keep quiet. If the group is trying to agree on something to do, I may express myself, but I'll usually follow the crowd.

I care about other people, and I'm sensitive to their needs. I'll pitch in and help when someone's got more than they can handle. I notice when they're angry or hurt, even at me, and will invite them to talk about it. I readily make myself available to my wife or friends or coworkers when they need to talk about a problem. When I worked in an office, I usually kept my door open and stopped whatever I was doing when anyone walked in. Overall, I feel like I'm a valuable member of society, the kind of guy people would want to have as their friend, neighbor, or coworker. I know other men feel that way too.

Passive Men Are Undefined

In his book *Iron John,* Robert Bly talks about "soft males," a synonym for passive men. "They're lovely, valuable people—I like them," he writes.

They're not interested in harming the earth or starting wars. There's a gentle attitude toward life in their whole being and style of living. But many of these men are not happy. You quickly notice the lack of energy in them. They are life-preserving but not exactly life-giving. Ironically, you often see these men with strong women who positively radiate energy.[1]

I can think of couples I've known who fit Bly's description. The woman leans forward in her chair, sharing about something that means a great deal to her. Her face is animated, her hands moving, her voice charged with feeling. Meanwhile, the man sits back on the couch, legs crossed, with one arm draped across the couchtop, nodding and smiling occasionally. He says very little, just enough to keep the conversation going, and seems terribly agreeable. I pick up nothing that would indicate he has any strong feelings or opinions about anything.

Whatever views he expresses are Politically Correct, guaranteed not to ruffle feathers. I note the startling contrast between these two people: The woman is full of energy and passion, unafraid to put out her feelings, willing to define herself in sharp, bold strokes. But I have no sense for who the man is, how he feels, what makes him tick; in fact, if I asked him, he probably wouldn't know what to say. I know because I've been like him before.

Passive Men Respond and React Rather than Initiate

Though I haven't played much lately, I'm good at ping-pong. If I can't beat you, I'll at least give you a run for your money. During high school, when I played the most, I adopted a largely defensive style. Rarely did I slam the ball, attempt fancy trick shots, or even come up with a game plan; instead, I simply learned to return whatever the other guy hit at me. I didn't know it, but my ping-pong strategy closely resembled my approach to life and relationships: sit back, go with the flow, don't set any agenda, respond only when something comes my way.

I found that this attitude stood out more clearly at home, with the significant others in my life, than it did at the office. On the job, I found it much easier to initiate ideas and assert myself, though I still needed people to remind me of deadlines. But each day in the car on the way home, a shift occurred, and by the time I walked in the door, I had all but abandoned my own initiative. For the rest of the evening I basically sat around and allowed my wife and son to set the agenda. Oh, I helped with dinner dishes, diaper changes, baths, and bedtime stories, but usually I had to be asked. My identity as a separate individual somehow vanished at home, or more accurately, merged with that of my first wife and son. After a few years of following this pattern, I began to feel uptight and unsettled during the evenings. I felt as if I had no control over my life and no time for myself. But rather than tap the creative energy I had at the office, express my need and propose a plan—a "cooling off" hour after work, regular times for me to "connect" with my son, perhaps a weekly night out for both spouses—I maintained the status quo until it was too late.

Not that the evening agenda in itself caused the breakdown of my first marriage. I saw plenty of other problems, both in my wife and in myself. But I seldom if ever brought them up, much less took responsibility for them. Again, I left the initiative up to my wife. And when she'd raise an issue or voice a frustration, I'd go into react-and-respond mode. Unfortunately, the unspoken question that guided me was not "How can I own and take responsibility for my side of this problem?" or "What feelings does this issue stir up in me?" but rather "How can I calm her down? How can I make her feel better?" The last two questions focus on the external, on someone else, while the first two direct me inward, to my center. Better yet, I could have taken the first step in recognizing the problem and expressed my own desire to work on it.

There are hundreds of ways that I have lived a life of responding rather than initiating, even today. Since I now work at home, the lines that separated job and home have blurred; some of my work initiative has leaked into home life, but some of my home passivity has also bled into my work. It's a lot harder for me to work when there's no boss and office schedule to give me structure; I now have to motivate myself from within, and I struggle with it every day. I still feel unsettled in the evenings at times, but I'm listening to myself much more nowadays and giving myself permission to read, write, watch a movie, attend a support group.

Another result of living by reacting is indecisiveness. At times I've been faced with difficult decisions that will offend someone no matter what. Rather than take a deep breath and choose the course that I know in my heart is best, I have all too often said, "Well, let's wait and see what happens." My vain hope is that something or someone else will cause the decision to be made so I don't appear to be the bad guy. It seems I can't stop fretting about what others will think of me.

Passive Men Feel a Vague Sense of Loss

When my first wife left me, I felt a sudden and terrible void, almost like the phantom pain amputees report. Because I had assumed that I was an incomplete person without a woman (while conveniently forgetting how unhappy I was while "complete"), I focused on my loss of her as the central problem. But what I didn't realize was that the greatest loss had taken place long before my first marriage had dissolved, and the loss had nothing to do with my first wife. What was it?

I didn't know, but I knew I'd lost it. I felt uneasy,

unsettled, unfulfilled. Perhaps I'd made the wrong career move. Maybe I'd married the wrong woman. Not until several years later did I learn that the loss had occurred within me. And the "it" I had lost was a sense of wholeness, vitality, and personhood within myself, apart from a relationship with a woman.

The feeling of loss may also tie into other things: loss of a potentially happy childhood; loss of a healthy relationship with your parents; loss of hopes and dreams you once had for yourself; loss of freedom and spontaneity you may have felt as a child; loss of the energy, strength, and endurance you once had in your body; or a general loss of passion and purpose in life. By obsessing on the loss of a woman, I managed to overlook these deeper losses that needed to be faced. I couldn't move forward in my growth until I had grieved over those losses, which represented large chunks of my self that had been hacked off early in life. In order for me to be whole, those lost parts needed to be reintegrated.

Passive Men Are Alienated

Closely related to loss is alienation, which men experience at many levels. Though the self is meant to operate as an integrated whole, we tend to break it up into isolated pieces such as mind, body, emotions, spirit, and soul. Then we set up an internal hierarchy of which pieces are most important, and focus on those, while ignoring, repressing, or denying the other parts. Some Christians I know practice a sort of modern-day Gnosticism by treating their "spiritual life" as if it were some other life than the one they live each day in their homes and in their jobs. Or they view Christianity as an intellectual pursuit rather than a dynamic, life-altering relationship with God. Their motives are pure, but they somehow miss out on the wholeness of life and personhood. The same is true, I believe, when people try to distinguish between a physical problem, an emotional problem, and a spiritual problem. Calling it one kind of problem immediately severs us from its other dimensions. Humans are multidimensional beings, yet we rarely focus on more than one part at a time.

Men especially have grown adept at neglecting essential parts of themselves, especially their feelings, instincts, and soul-stirrings. In Western society we men have chosen to live primarily in one dimension: the head, the highest part of the body. For a variety of reasons, beginning with the Enlightenment but accelerating in this century, we have elevated the activities we associate with the head—thinking, reasoning, logic, intellect, facts—to a position of supremacy in our lives, allowing them to act as dictator over the rest of our person.

From an early age I learned to live in my head. I found that my parents approved of me when I was nice, and disapproved when I wasn't. The learning came through trial and error at first—hugs and praise for being "good," a slap on the mouth if I "talked back," affirmation for refusing to fight with a neighbor kid who picked on me mercilessly, a whack on the butt if I got too energetic indoors. As I grew older, I realized it took hard work to be nice. I had to suppress all my other un-nice feelings such as anger, jealousy, hurt, and disappointment. And I could only do it by rerouting those feelings through my head, where I could analyze and rationalize them away. *I shouldn't be angry because he didn't really mean what he said. If I hadn't started it he wouldn't have said that to me. It's really my fault because I made a mistake. Dad had a hard day at work today so I shouldn't say anything. If I act grumpy I won't get to play football with the other kids.*

It wasn't long before my head was working overtime to keep my niceness intact and hold down everything else. I also learned that niceness was closely related to performance, and that I could earn approval by performing well in school. So I strove for good grades and found that by achieving academically I could please both my parents and my teachers, as well as gain some respect from other students. This took even more headwork on my part. Not until I developed an ulcer in college and skin rashes a few years later did it occur to me that I was ignoring and abusing the other parts of my self by living constantly in my head. I spent so much time trying to figure out what other people wanted from me that I had little energy left to listen to my own wants and needs.

So many men today use their heads in this one-dimensional way. We dismiss our feelings as irrational, not to be trusted. We seek medical treatment for bodily pain, but seldom examine whether emotional and spiritual factors are causing the pain. Instead, we go for a little more exercise, a little less stress, or a little less fat in our diet, and we take Excedrin, Valium, or Tums to trick the body into assuming it's not hurting. There is a certain disjointedness to our life: things that should be connected aren't. We act decisively at the office and fade into the woodwork at home. We climax during lovemaking even when we don't feel great passion at the moment. (Or we fail to climax and can't understand why.) We calmly say nothing's wrong when we are boiling on the inside. We wish we could be a musician or a photographer, but instead we program computers. We say we believe in God, perhaps even from the pulpit of a church, yet we feel little if anything of his presence in our lives. We can see evidence, of course—an occasional answered prayer, a quickly ended sickness, a narrowly avoided accident—but we don't feel the person of God dwelling within us.

All of this adds up to an overwhelming sense of alienation—within ourselves and between ourselves and others. Somehow the Christian belief that "God has combined the members of the body . . . so that there should be no division in the body, but that its parts should have equal concern for each other" (1 Corinthians 12:24–25) goes out the window. We believe it in our head, but not in our entire body. And rather than search for ways to reconnect the body and the head, we settle for being stuck in the skull.

Passive Men Don't Know How to Relate to Other Men

Passive men are not only alienated from their bodies and feelings; they are also estranged from each other. I recall feeling a quasi-camaraderie with some of my male coworkers on the school newspaper staffs in high school and college, but it centered primarily on completing a task. As an adult, I never had a problem getting together with other men to do something—a movie, a concert, a remodeling project, a softball game—but I found it difficult to share my feelings and struggles with them, and so did they with me.

For five summers I played on the park-district softball team. Every Saturday we would laugh and sweat and yell and slap each other on the back for two hours—like in the Miller beer commercials. We joked about our jobs in a superficial way, but it was a rare moment that I got to know anything about my teammates beneath the veneer of noise, competition, and bravado. I enjoyed myself, but it was fun, not intimacy, that I experienced.

The closest thing I ever felt to intimacy with other men occurred between me and my coworkers in the magazine business. Again, most of it was work—and task-oriented— but I believe our connection extended partially into the spiritual and emotional level. We could talk occasionally about struggles we were having in our marriages or with our children. Even with these longtime male friends, however, deeper sharing seldom came naturally. And we rarely got together outside of the office.

Over my entire life, I can think of no more than a half-dozen men with whom I could verbalize my feelings and who could share their with me. Most men I know wouldn't be able to name that many. What has caused this emotional distance between men? Undoubtedly part of the reason is that men have a much harder time knowing what their feelings are in the first place. Since day one, it seems, boys have been told to be strong and tough, not to cry or show any signs of "weakness," especially around other boys. By the time these boys reach adulthood, society has trained them to stuff down their feelings long before they reach the surface. But there are other factors too. Maybe it's the rampant homophobia in our culture: So many men, under the surface, are terrified that others may think they're homosexual, or worse, that they might even *be* homosexual, that they won't risk closeness with another man. Perhaps the most important reason is that sons of the past few generations have generally had greater access to the listening ear and the encircling arms of their mothers rather than their fathers. With no father available to share with at the feeling level, it's no wonder men have trouble relating to each other.

Though my father was physically present for me in some ways, he was absent emotionally. I needed affirmation and encouragement from him, and somehow didn't get enough. Consequently I felt a sense of betrayal, suspicion, and distrust around him. As I grew into young adulthood, I unwittingly allowed my suspicion to extend to older men and authority figures in general. *What do they know? They're out of touch and they don't care about people like me anyway,* I'd conclude. In fact, many older men are out of touch. But not all of them. Some have gone through the long and difficult process of coming to terms with *their* absent fathers and have acquired a wisdom and depth that can serve as a model for younger men.

Passive Men Avoid Responsibility

When I was a magazine editor, I used to enjoy keeping my office door open so I could be available to coworkers who had questions or simply wanted to say hello. It helped staff relationships and morale, I told myself. But often my open-door policy kept me from completing my work and meeting deadlines, because I was allowing other people to dictate how my time was used. At the end of the day, when I looked at the pile of unfinished reports and unanswered mail on my desk, I had a built-in excuse: Hey, Bob needed to talk to me about a problem—what could I do? What I could have done was close my door at times, or set aside certain hours to be available, so I would be able to finish my own work. But deep down I knew I was using Bob to avoid taking responsibility for what I needed to do.

Or take being nice. I've found that niceness goes a long way toward making the world a better place. I enjoy being nice. But I've realized that so often when I don't feel nice inside, I still act nice on the outside. I avoid telling the truth. I don't want to be mean to people, but on the other hand, do I always need to answer "fine" when someone asks how I am? Why can't I be real and say what I'm feeling, communicating as much as is appropriate for the person I'm talking to? When my wife, Nancy, asks how I'm feeling, she's not just making small talk; she really wants to know. But all too often I have used "fine" to close myself off from her and others, rather than share myself; and the more I do it, the more I close off from myself. By automatically saying "fine," I don't have to ask myself how I feel, especially if under the surface I'm not feeling so great. It's a way of avoiding responsibility to myself.

I feel this avoidance even more keenly when I know I need to confront someone—my wife, my son, a relative, a coworker. One of them may have said or done something (intentionally or not) that hurt or angered me. Sometimes

I'm hardly even aware that I have a feeling about what happened. In a very real way, I'm being passive to my own hurt, not caring enough about it (that is, my self) to pay attention to the feeling. I turn gray inside and walk around in sort of a fog. More recently, though, I feel the hurt or anger rising inside me, and I realize that I must make a choice: to express or ignore myself, to face conflict or avoid it.

Avoiding is almost always related to pain. We are tempted to avoid things that are painful—physically or emotionally. I avoid completing my work because I'm afraid of having to make some difficult decisions, or I'm worried that I won't do a good enough job and will be criticized. I avoid speaking up about being angry because I'm afraid people won't like me any more, or that it will erode my relationship with my wife or my son. So I resort to some kind of behavior that enables me to bypass my pain. "Some of us will go to quite extraordinary lengths to avoid our problems and the suffering they cause," M. Scott Peck writes in *The Road Less Traveled,* "proceeding far afield from all that is clearly good and sensible in order to try to find an easy way out."[2] Passivity is going for the easy way out, suppressing the truth and shifting our growth.

Passive Men Struggle with Addictions or Compulsions

To avoid the pain of our problems we may resort to substances, habits, or behaviors that appear to make life more manageable but actually separate us further from our true identity. Addictions to alcohol, drugs, work, food, women, sex, sports, money, and gadgets often serve to mask the deeper feelings of pain, loss, and longing that lie within us.

My substances of choice over the years have been sugar and caffeine. While these may not have the same potential for personal destruction as alcohol or cocaine, they still contributed to a cycle of dependency and self-denial for me. About five years ago I drank so much Pepsi that I found myself planning my schedule around it. I would drink it first thing in the morning. I changed my driving route to work so I could stop at 7-Eleven and pick up a Super Big Gulp. Then, over the course of the day, I'd still drink the equivalent of a six-pack, and there was still the evening left. I'd even plan some of my meals according to how well the foods "went with" Pepsi. When I got into a jam, I'd grab a Pepsi. When I felt angry, depressed, or hurting, I'd reach for another can. I told myself I needed it to clear my head, to help me focus on the project I needed to finish, to help me stay awake when I worked late. Then, after all that caffeine, I had trouble getting to sleep at night. I'd wake the next morning with less sleep than I needed, and the cycle would begin again.

During that period, I was using so much of my energy to feed my addiction that I had little left to confront the inner struggles I was facing—the feelings of pain and hurt and failure over a recently crumbled marriage, the lack of purpose and direction in my life, and my seeming inability to know who I was as a man.

Addictions to substances or food are only a part of the picture, however. The growth of Twelve-Step support groups such as Adult Children of Alcoholics (ACOA) and Codependents Anonymous (CoDA) has shown that many behavior patterns can have the same effect on a person and those around him as an actual substance addiction. For example, those who spend excessive time working, who easily fly into a rage, who obsess about sex or women or masturbation, or who break off relationships frequently are probably caught in compulsive patterns of living that prevent them from experiencing their deeper, truer selves. In a way, passivity itself is a form of addiction, because it is a habitual turning away from one's own needs and feelings and a focusing on (or reacting to) the actions or words of others. In the lingo of recovery, it would be known as *codependency*.

Passive Men Don't Know How to Get Angry

I've already said we have trouble getting in touch with our feelings, but anger stands out as a particularly difficult emotion to handle. Over the past few generations, many men have been storing layer upon layer of unexpressed anger in their muscles and bones and organs. It may be anger at their absent or abusive fathers, anger at a government that sent them off to a war they didn't believe in, anger at a fundamentalist religious system that squashed their personhood, anger at an oppressive and demeaning employer. Unfortunately, Western society has provided no significant outlet for men to express anger firmly and forthrightly, yet without being violent or domineering.

When I feel anger, I usually go for one of two extremes: shove it down completely and say nothing, or resort to shouting, judging, and defiance. I may hold it in because I'm afraid of being rejected, abandoned, labeled, or criticized; because I'm afraid of the feeling itself, that it will be too big or monstrous and I'll lose control; because I don't want to hurt the other person's feelings; because I know it won't change anything; because I know I won't get my way anyway; or some other reason. For me, all of these excuses boil down to believing that my anger (that is, my self) doesn't matter enough to be expressed forthrightly. Put another way, I allow the external results, what goes on outside of me, to matter more than what's happening inside of me.

On the other end of the spectrum, when I do try to let my anger out, often what comes out is not anger but hostility, judgment, and condemnation of the other person. With Nancy, I usually point my finger at her parentally and say things like, "You always . . . !" and "You never . . . !" I make everything into a black-and-white, good-and-bad, right-and-wrong issue, and aggressively try to prove that I'm right and she's wrong. And before I know it, I've bypassed the anger and gone back up into my head again, where I can analyze, formulate arguments, recall evidence, put together a case, and stay on safe but useless territory.

Actually these two extremes go hand in hand, because the flip side of passive is aggressive. If we hold our anger down too long, as so many men have done, eventually it can erupt in a vicious barrage of judgment. Sometimes just a little bit of the anger escapes in the form of sarcastic remarks, jokes at someone else's expense, lack of sexual interest, an anniversary conveniently forgotten. Or the anger can be transferred to others—the dog, the driver who cut you off, the restaurant with no nonsmoking section.

Whichever direction my anger goes, neither of these extremes is honest, healthy, or honoring to myself or the other person. I'm either withholding myself or exploding, and neither is a true expression of me. Both approaches are passive because they avoid the truth and because they depend on other people or external results rather than on my own needs and choices. My frustration has been that I never learned a middle ground. I never learned to listen to my anger, own it, express it clearly and directly, and then let it lie there, possibly as a starting point for dialogue, possibly not. I always thought I had to use my anger to change other people, to prove them wrong, to judge them. Only recently have I begun to realize that anger occurs within me, and that the primary value in expressing it is in honoring me, that is, myself in all my fullness. And I can truly honor others only when I have first honored myself.

Passive Men Allow Themselves to Be Entranced by Women

For most of my life, I have been mysteriously driven by a few certain beliefs about women, though I've never been able to articulate them until recently. First, I've had this overwhelming sense that all the greatest things I want in life—growth into wholeness as a person, happiness, meaning, fulfillment, even spiritual salvation—would somehow come through a woman. I could not experience these things on my own; I simply had to have the presence, the help, the reassurance, and the support of a woman to be whole. (I also assumed women must have a similar view about men.) How did this unconscious conviction express itself? From ninth grade onward, I made sure I had a girlfriend or a steady date, because then I could say I was "with" someone, that I was complete, I was okay. The quality of the relationship didn't concern me nearly as much as being in the relationship.

When I paired off with a woman, I placed her up on a pedestal and envisioned her as possessing all kinds of magical powers and ideal traits. She would instinctively know my needs and move to fill them. She would joyfully compensate for all my weaknesses. She would always be warm and affectionate, always make me feel better, always make my problems and stresses go away. However, when she fell off the pedestal, which she did often because she was a human and not a goddess, I overlooked it. Or else I believed I had pushed her off, and blamed myself. In either case, I'd pick her up and put her back in her place on the pedestal. Never did I try to view the women I went out with as real people with their own separate needs and hurts and desires; I could only see them in terms of their relationship to me. Nor did I make a serious effort to find out who I was as a separate person, apart from a woman. It's a lot like being in a trance or under a spell: I'm blindly pursuing a fantasy that constantly eludes me, all the while ignoring the stark reality around me.

A second aspect to my trance was that I admired strong women, mostly from a distance. They seemed to be so in control of their lives, standing up for themselves and going for what they wanted. It somehow escaped me that these traits were the very ones I lacked—and desperately wanted—in myself; instead, I thought I was progressive and liberated because I liked a woman who wasn't a submissive dishrag. But nearly all my admiration came from afar— these women for some reason seemed unapproachable, unattainable. I also found myself drawn to music by gutsy, macho-female vocalists like Pat Benatar and Heart.

The third aspect to my trance was most disturbing. Whenever conflict arose between me and a significant woman in my life, I felt powerless to prevail over her. Usually I gave in without even thinking, and often without minding. But sometimes I realized I would have to give up something I really wanted, and then I'd put up a fuss. I might rave and fume and protest, but in the end I'd give in every time. It wasn't so much winning that mattered as having to forgo what I wanted. When it came to a showdown, I had the overwhelming sense that there was no choice but to give in. I could only get my way with her permission. There never seemed to be any middle ground, no room for dialogue or negotiation. I never knew how to make my needs and desires known in a clear, authentic, forthright way, expressing from my deeper self, "This is me, this is who I am, this is what I need right now." All I could do was stay in my head and try to prove that what I wanted was right or logical. But ultimately I knew it was fruitless: Sooner or later my wants and needs, and even my self, would be swallowed up by the great goddess.

At times my frustration has been so great that I would even say I felt victimized by women. This may strike a few men and many women as a harsh and unfair statement, especially after all the centuries of domination women have had to endure at the hands of men. There is a key difference, however: Most of the men today who feel victimized by women—including me—have brought it upon themselves by handing too much of their own power over to women.

I wondered if this trancelike feeling was just me, or if others had it too. I asked a number of my male friends, and to my surprise they immediately said they felt the same. We all had a preoccupation with women in one way or another. If only we could get our relationships with women worked out, or if only we could find the right woman or get our woman back, then life would be manageable and fulfilling. The more we talked about it, the more I knew we had all fallen under a spell.

Passive Men Say Yes Too Often

Because we depend on the approval and acceptance of others for our sense of well-being, we are quick to say yes when we're asked, especially by women, to do things. In a way we treat "yes" a lot like "fine," because we so often say it automatically, without stopping to ask ourselves, Do I want to do this? Do I need to do this? Does this fit for me?

I virtually defined myself by the word yes in high school and college. I said yes to the school paper, yes to the yearbook, yes to the school musical, yes to the student council, yes to the Key Club, yes to the tennis team, yes to the college choir, yes to teaching a Sunday school class, yes to helping with the church youth group. I was so desperate for external approval that I jumped at every chance I could find to impress people with my performance. And if the performance itself was less than overwhelming, people would still be impressed by how busy and active I was. I handled my commitments in the same way airlines overbook passengers: I said yes to them all, and then assumed a few would fall through the cracks. If they didn't, I'd beg my way out at the last minute and then owe them a favor. As a result, I overextended myself on behalf of others and had no time left to invest in my own soul-growth.

I have always found it hard to tell someone no in person, probably because I feared they'd interpret it as rejection and then turn around and reject me. Rather than say, "No, I won't be able to make it," or "I'll have to think about it," I'd just say yes and then later leave a message with the person's secretary or on their answering machine. In raising my son, Brendan, I avoided saying no as much as possible because I didn't want to hurt or stifle him—so I told myself—when actually my motive was that I wanted him to like me. But by saying yes, I was avoiding the truth, being indirect, and running from responsibility. I was being passive.

The issue of saying yes comes up frequently in the workplace, where bosses or coworkers give out assignments or make requests. Some of these may be unreasonable, unfair, too difficult, poorly timed, hurtful to others or the environment, or morally questionable. Most any job requires a certain amount of give and take, and at least an occasional nod to office politics, but is it always necessary to "just do my job" or "do what I'm told"? Too often men fail to stand up for their convictions and their personhood. Or they don't ask specifically for what they need to achieve excellence and integrity in their work. Instead, they do whatever keeps the boss and the company happy. They become Yes-men, with no mind or soul of their own.

Perhaps the best example of Yes-men in today's society can be found in so many of our country's politicians—conservatives and liberals alike—who by saying yes to scads of special-interest groups have left our government in disarray, devoid of vision and conscience. By and large, our country is being run by passive men who don't want to offend anyone by saying no.

Passive Men Have Difficulty Setting and Defending Their Boundaries

Passive men find it hard to set and maintain clear boundaries. An individual self can be compared to a house. A man (or any person) with a reasonably clear sense of self knows when to open and close the doors to his house. He invites certain people to enter and forbids others who may harm him or tempt him or steal his valuables. At times he may want time for himself, or he may want to clean or redecorate the house, so he closes the door for a while, until he is ready to open it again. Closed doors also protect him from arctic winds and violent rainstorms, while open doors welcome the sunshine and balmy breezes. It's important to note that the man who knows and cares for his own self *chooses* which doors to open and close and when. The choice also applies to doors within the house.

A passive man leaves the doors to his self-house standing open. Or maybe he's allowed them to be removed altogether. As a result, people can enter at any time and stay as long as they want, even people with harmful intentions, or people that hinder the man's growth. The man may keep the exterior nicely painted and the lawn groomed, but inside the house is mostly empty. Most everything of value has been stolen, and what's left has been damaged or vandalized. Stormy weather blows unhindered through the doors and windows, wreaking further havoc. The passive man seems to have lost, or given up, his power to choose when to open and close the doors of his house. Often the problem begins with childhood boundary violations through physical or emotional abuse.

For life to be focused and purposeful, we need to establish various kinds of boundaries around ourselves and within ourselves. These boundaries define the edges of our selves—who we are and who we are not, what we desire for our life and what we do not, what we believe and don't believe, what is our responsibility and what is not, what is our feeling or opinion and what is someone else's, what we will tolerate and what we will not, and so on. Boundaries need to be strong enough to withstand attack, yet flexible enough to be adjusted if we gain new insight into ourselves.

Some men, for instance, find themselves pulled head-long into unhealthy or extramarital relationships with women, as if by a mysterious force. For some reason they are unable to maintain a boundary line of discretion between themselves and other women. Others may have trouble drawing the line between their job and their family, always bringing paperwork home in the evenings and taking along a stuffed briefcase on family vacations. Men who can't say no are struggling with boundary issues.

I have not sufficiently protected my boundaries when I frequently allow people, events, and circumstances "to get to me." I have trouble remaining separate from other people's ideas, feelings, opinions, and judgments. Like a house with all the doors open, everything flows freely in and out, so I can't sort out other people's feelings from my own. Someone may criticize me, and instead of keeping separate and asking myself how it fits with my own perception, I immediately respond (verbally or nonverbally), "You're right, I blew it. I'm no good. I'm sorry." Or if Nancy happens to be feeling down, I have trouble standing back and letting her be down. I feel like I have to stop being in a good mood and be down too, or that I have to jump in and try to fix her feelings. I even have trouble with the interior doors of my self-house at times. When I'm working, for instance, I find that I'm easily distracted and can't concentrate. Another way of saying it is that I haven't been able to set a clear enough work boundary and defend it from intrusions.

Not setting boundaries is passive because it gives over the care and control of our life to other people, events, or circumstances. It means we are surrendering our power to make our own choices.

OUTSIDE IN

So many men today have no idea who they are on the inside, underneath the various roles they prop themselves up with. And since Western culture at the end of the twentieth century has called many of those roles into question anyway, men have even less structure to support their wobbly exterior. More and more of them are resorting to the passive approach to living I've described above, an approach that basically says, "Well, if I don't know who I am, then I'll just be whatever X wants me to be." (Fill in the appropriate word for X: my wife, my mother, my father, my church, my boss, my kids, my ethnic group, the market, all of the above.)

At their core, passive men have lost touch with their core; whatever core we have is buried deep within our psyche. And rather than go inside to find that essential, interior self, we have settled for a substitute: the expectations, rules, behavior patterns, verdicts, and needs of others. We're living from the outside in rather than from the inside out.

In the poem that follows, a friend of mine who is an actor captured the emptiness of living from the outside in rather than from the inside out. Though he speaks as an actor, he depicts the state of so many passive men:

Roaming with a Hungry Heart

So many times I've stood there,
Spouting words of other men
Whose hearts I found a kinship with,
Now I sit and look inside for something of my own—
And find that I am barren and devoid;
An actor in search of a character,
Reflecting other men's thoughts and feelings,

But with none that are mine.
And so it seems in so many other ways,
I'm always searching for what I lack within—
Or perhaps merely don't recognize—
A friend, a lover, or an artist,
Who will be
Whatever I can't find in me.

—Joseph Rose

When we simply play the roles everyone else expects of us, we're not happy, whole, or fulfilled. The women in our lives are frustrated with us, even though we've been trying to please them. We don't feel connected to God, even though we may be going through the motions of spirituality.

What needs to happen? What do passive men need to do? What steps can we take? I've been asking these questions myself. Initially, I figured it only makes sense that the way to stop being passive is to be active, right? Get disciplined, establish a routine, form a plan, and get busy?

As I've begun my own journey out of passivity, I've found that what I need to do first is nothing. I've been so conditioned to believe that *doing* is the answer to everything, that what I do is who I am, and what I do is what will change me. It isn't, and it won't. If I really want to find my self, my identity as a man, I must learn not to do, but to *be*. Only when I allow myself to be, to be still, to be alone with myself, can I begin to discover and listen to my own desires, yearnings, heart-hungers, wounds, feelings, and passions. These are the stuff of the self, the substance of the soul.

Odd as it may seem, this kind of "inactivity" is the farthest thing from passivity. Trained as we are to stay busy, setting goals, making plans, writing to-do lists, checking off chores as they're done, we often trick ourselves into believing that our external activities really are all there is to life. This can even be true for people "in recovery" or in some other program for emotional/spiritual growth. Such a person may think, *If I go to three meetings each week, attend*

George Guru's seminar, take two retreats, and read five books,
then I'll grow spiritually and find my identity. The Christian
may say, *If I study my Bible and pray every day, keep a prayer*
list, go to church twice a week, and read J. I. Packer's Knowing
God, *then I'll grow spiritually and find my true identity.* To
both people my answer would be, *Don't count on it.*

All of these activities can be a valuable part of our
growth and our search for identity. But they'll have little
benefit unless we allow some empty space between the
things we *do* to reflect on who we *are,* what we're learning,
how we're feeling, what has changed or not changed, what
we really want and need. It is in these empty spaces, rather
than in all the noise and busyness, that we men are more
likely to hear the voice of God, and of our deeper self.

At one point in his life, the biblical prophet Elijah felt
defeated and depressed, and needed God's assurance and
guidance. From his hiding place in a mountain cave, he cried
out to God. According to the story (1 Kings 19:11–12),
God revealed himself to Elijah in an interesting way:

> Then a great and powerful wind tore the mountains
> apart and shattered the rocks before the Lord, but the
> Lord was not in the wind. After the wind there was an
> earthquake, but the Lord was not in the earthquake. After
> the earthquake came a fire, but the Lord was not in the
> fire. And after the fire came a gentle whisper.

Not in all the fire and fury, but in a gentle whisper did
Elijah come face-to-face with God. So also do today's men
need to create spaces in their lives where they can listen for
God's gentle whisper. Quieting down the din of all our
activity is not easy, and it most certainly is not passive; it
takes hard work. Even after the space is created, an active
form of listening is required to hear the voices from God
and from within ourselves that will lead us out of passivity
and toward our true identity as men.

Two

Men and the Wound

Struggling in my father's hands,
Striving against my swadling bands,
Bound and weary, I thought best
To sulk upon my mother's breast.

—William Blake

Passivity finds its origins in a wound.

As young children, we experience the world—at least for a while or in scattered moments—as a vast, awesome, wonderful place, and we want to touch, taste, try out, and explore everything. There is a lightness to our being, a sense of freedom, of spontaneity, of immediacy, of unity. We make no distinction between our bodies and our feelings, between our own needs and those of others, between learning and play. Most of us would count these childhood moments of bliss as among the happiest days of our lives.

But at those moments of fullness, and indeed throughout the first twenty years of life, we are also extremely vulnerable to hurt. Before long we find that the world doesn't always like us the way we are, and it reacts. Some of these reactions are necessary and help us to survive and grow. But sometimes the actions and words of others (or lack thereof) have an adverse effect on us, injuring our bodies or souls and obstructing our growth. These are the wounds of childhood, the wounds that lead to passivity.

We can be emotionally or physically wounded by many sources, and in all sorts of ways, some intentional, some inadvertent. Wounds can come from people, such as our parents, siblings, relatives, teachers, coaches, employers, peers. They can come from the culture, subculture, socio-economic or ethnic group we are a part of. They can come from systems, governments, or institutions. They can even come from nature, as in the flood or tornado that destroyed our house, physical impairments, learning disabilities, major

49

illnesses in us or our family. And finally wounds can come from (for lack of a better word) fate, or whatever it is that causes us or someone close to us to be seriously injured in an accident or by a random act of violence, terrorism, or war. The kinds of wounds I am speaking of may or may not be physical, but they will always be emotional, significantly damaging our inner perceptions of ourselves, others, and the world. Unless we can identify these wounds, face them, and allow them to transform us, we will remain their victim and continue to be caught in our passivity.

Several kinds of wounds have particularly affected men in the past century: the wounds of today's industrialized culture, the wounds of the absent father, and the wounds of the too-present mother.

THE TECHNO-WOUND

I suppose it's possible to claim that male passivity began with Adam in the Garden of Eden, who tried to blame Eve for his problems rather than take responsibility for them. But most of the social commentary on the current male identity crisis begins with the Industrial Revolution of the mid-1800s. It's a good place to start, because it marks the time that fathers all over the country left their homes and farms for jobs in the factories. The effect on their sons was to deprive them of a day-by-day model for manhood. Before we look at the sons, however, I want to examine industry's effects on our society as a whole, and then on society's fathers.

One word that characterizes the spirit of mechanization is *automatic,* literally "self-moving." Something that was automatic moved, worked, or performed some task by itself, eliminating the need for a person to do the moving or perform the task. A machine by nature requires less of us. It ends up doing the meaningful activity on its own, leaving us merely to push the buttons and keep the machines in good working order. The result is to remove us from the creative act; our role has shifted from an active to a passive one.

An automated factory could produce many times more tables or chairs or coats than people could make on their own, and it required fewer workers. But these plants could also manufacture products that were themselves automatic, which required less of the consumers who purchased them. Automatic washers, dryers, dishwashers, stoves, refrigerators, lawn mowers, and cars led us increasingly to believe that the good life meant sitting back and letting machines do our work for us. We also became enthralled with anything labeled "instant"—from instant pudding to instant coffee to instant cameras.

Instant meant that we didn't have to go through a process to get what we wanted; we could achieve final results without the work. So we bought all our foods and our fibers already processed. No more mixing, peeling, soaking, boiling. No more hand washing, line drying, or ironing. And so on with product after product. Somehow the effect of all of this was to remove our sense of participation in the world, and therefore our sense of responsibility. We became passive.

At present the computer stands at the pinnacle of so-called progress; we tend to place more trust in things that are computer-made or computer-controlled. But we also tend to expect these products to take over all our responsibilities.

One night last summer Nancy and I went to a movie not far from our home along the Hudson River in New York. The theater was freezing, and I asked the manager standing in back if she could turn down the air conditioning. "Sorry, there isn't much I can do," she said, "because our heating and cooling are controlled by a computer in Dallas, Texas."

I came across some words recently that capture the

essence of what happens when we give ourselves over to machines:

> When a man uses a machine he carries on all his business in a machine-like manner. Whoever does his business in the manner of a machine develops a machine heart. Whoever has a machine heart in his breast loses his simplicity. Whoever loses his simplicity becomes uncertain in the impulses of his spirit. Uncertainty in the impulses of the spirit is something that is incompatible with truth.[1]

Not only was I struck by the truth of these words written by Chinese sage Chang Tsi, but by the time in which they were written—2,500 years ago. Mechanization has not only turned us into a culture of passivity; it has made us "uncertain in the impulses of the spirit." We have lost touch with our spiritual center and, therefore, with God. We don't know who we are anymore, so we look outside of ourselves, to machines, to structures, to external trappings, to define who we are. I'm not saying technology is bad or that we should return to a pre-industrial state to find ourselves; rather, that we've allowed technology to tear out our inner sense of identity and responsibility. Unless we see what has happened to us and take the time and make the effort to consciously reclaim our inner spiritual identity, we will never escape passivity.

As the twentieth century draws to a close, we find ourselves living in a post-industrialized society, one in which we are even further removed from active, meaningful work. Jobs consist more and more of pushing paper, entering, sorting, and analyzing data, buying and selling things that don't really exist, such as junk bonds, credit holdings, and stock futures. Corporations grow not by producing more goods but by taking over other companies. It all has a numbing effect on our personhood.

Perhaps no aspect of our techno-culture has contributed to our passivity like the entertainment industry, especially television and movies. While I refuse to launch into a tirade against these forces—I'm a great fan of some TV shows and I love going to the movies—I also recognize the damage they've done to me and to our society. First of all, they make us sit in one place and do nothing. We become passive absorbers of whatever the screen is feeding us. The only active thing we can do is change the channel with the remote control or eat microwave popcorn. I used to think that movies were a tad less passive than TV, since I at least had to get in the car and drive to a movie theater; but with the pervasiveness of VCRs and cable TV, even that tiny distinction has vanished. I don't need the theaters for most films any more—I can see them on HBO or wait for the video.

There is a second, more insidious way that movies and TV reinforce our passivity. Today's entertainment business has fallen under the same spell as the rest of our mechanized society. It too wants to make products that are automatic or instant. So when we turn on the TV, we watch complex personal and social problems get solved in a half-hour drama, or at most, a two-hour movie. The amazing nonreality of shows featuring lawyers (*L.A. Law, Matlock,* and the Perry Mason movies, for example) has struck me lately, since we all know the legal system can grind away on a single case for months and years rather than minutes. But no matter. Even though we know these dramas don't mirror real life, our steady diet of them still creates expectations that our own problems can be solved and our own growth achieved this quickly and easily. When it doesn't happen, we feel disappointed, powerless, and we give up too easily on ourselves. We forget that a long, sometimes boring and difficult process must go on between the highlight scenes of life. And as long as we try to skip the process and jump right to the chase, we are being passive.

A third way the entertainment media reinforce passivity

is by making life on the screen infinitely more exciting and interesting than the comparatively boring lives we live each day. Since the industrial boom has already yanked us away from meaningful activity and work, Hollywood tries to compensate by portraying people of great power and influence, of decisive action, people who reach their dreams, bring about justice, and make a difference in the world. If we cannot find meaning and fulfillment in our own life, through TV and film we'll at least be able to experience it secondhand in someone else's life. Again, we are trained to shut down our own needs, hurts, desires, and dreams, and look outside of ourselves to discover who we are. Hello passivity.

Not only has the content of the entertainment media pushed us toward passivity, but also the advertising that clogs all the commercial breaks. If there is any one message most advertising communicates, it is that we can satisfy inner emotional and spiritual needs with external, material goods. Feeling afraid and insecure around people? Don't bother to face your fear and explore its underlying causes; just buy the right kind of makeup, toothpaste, mouthwash, or deodorant. Or fork out for a weight-loss program, a facelift, a hair transplant, or a tummy tuck.

The changes begun by the Industrial Revolution have also led us to take a passive view of our religious faith. More and more we treat religion as simply another product that should automatically do something for us when we're in a jam or need answers. For many of us, faith is limited to an external body of propositions and rules that can be classified, studied, quantified, analyzed, accepted, or reject-ed. It can so easily become an abstract, intellectual exercise. We get so preoccupied with the externals that we miss faith's larger, inner dimension, as a wonderfully mysterious experience of God personally dwelling deep within us, transforming us from the inside out.

All too often, we go to church with the same attitude with which we go to a concert: We sit through "performances" by the minister, the choir, and the organist, and evaluate them afterward in the manner of Siskel and Ebert. And many churches, sensing this mindset in their parishioners, opt for flashier, slicker Sunday services. Some feature a dazzling musical repertoire; others secure a big-name Bible expositor; and still others boast of a huge, state-of-the-art facility with plush seating so we can be comfortable during the show. Amidst all the fanfare, it rarely occurs to us that going to church can be an opportunity to participate in the spiritual redemption of the whole world, including ourselves and our families. Instead, we settle for a passive religion that (we hope) will do everything for us. All we have to do is sit back, enjoy, and wait for results. And if the performance doesn't give us the lift we want, we simply change churches or drop organized religion altogether.

Carl Jung noticed this trend toward the external in religion years ago. He explains it this way:

> For [modern man] the various forms of religion no longer appear to come from within, from the psyche; they seem more like items from the inventory of the outside world. No spirit not of this world vouchsafes him inner revelation; instead, he tries on a variety of religions and beliefs as if they were Sunday attire, only to lay them aside again like worn-out clothes.[2]

Another devastating consequence of industrialization is that a man's relationship to the earth—as old as man himself—has been severed. For thousands of years men have been tillers of the soil, living and working in tune with the rhythms, cycles, and seasons of the earth. Men invested themselves in the earth, caring for it, nurturing it, preserving it, because they knew firsthand that its fruits were their source of life. In a real way, part of a man's identity lay in his relationship to the land. The original meaning of the word husband, for example, included not only a man's commit-

ment to his wife, children, and home, but also his steward-
ship over the land they lived upon. With the rise of
industrialization and the end of a man's daily, ongoing
relationship with the earth, this fuller understanding of
being a husband—and a man—fell by the wayside. Yet we
still retain the less frequently used terms husbandman ("one
that plows and cultivates land: farmer") and husbandry ("the
control or judicious use of resources: conservation; the
cultivation or production of plants and animals"), which now
refer only to those for whom working the land is a career.

But not only have men been cut off from the earth, they
have in many cases been turned against it. The factories
these men worked in required vast quantities of raw
materials—trees, coal, minerals, oil—which led to large-
scale scalping of forests and hillsides with little or no
thought to their environmental effect. And after the raw
materials were processed, these plants dumped tons of
waste, much of it toxic, into the country's streams and
rivers, and spewed it into the air. The men who worked in
these factories felt, at least unconsciously, guilty and
powerless about what they were doing to the earth, while
the men who managed the companies usually denied
responsibility.

If a man's identity is (at least in part) tied to the earth,
what happens to him when our technological society tears
him away from the earth, perhaps even forces him to abuse
it? Something in the man is killed, I think, or at the very
least paralyzed. As our involvement with nature and its
rhythms stops, our awareness of being part of a world much
larger than ourself is numbed; we are unable to be
nourished and taught by the land, unable to see the
handiwork of God in the earth, and therefore unable to act
effectively as its stewards. To be paralyzed and frozen,
raping the earth when our soul is saying no, is to be passive.

So far we've seen some of the roots of passivity in our

automated culture. Technology and its related socioeconomic ripples have affected everyone, male and female, old and young, religious and nonreligious; and while in some ways it has made our lives easier, in other ways it has robbed us of our creative core, our active, vital self. This theft by technology inflicts a wound to our soul, a wound every bit as real as a knife-stab in the chest. In particular, the wound to our society's fathers and their sons is especially deep.

How badly are today's men hurting from these societal wounds? Andrew Kimbrell, attorney and policy director for the Washington, D.C.-based Foundation on Economic Trends, collected some startling figures on the state of men in American culture.[3] The suicide rate among men overall is four times that of women, and the life expectancy of men is 10 percent shorter. Men account for two-thirds of all alcoholics, 90 percent of all arrests for alcohol and drug abuse violations, 80 percent of our country's homeless, and 60 percent of high school dropouts. Among minority men, the statistics are even worse: Black males have the lowest life expectancy of all segments of the population. More than half of all black boys are raised without their fathers. There are more black men in jail than in college, and 40 percent more black women go to college than black men. Among blacks in the 20-to-29 age group, ten times as many men as women (one in four) are either in jail, on probation, or on parole. Together these data show the despair and desperation so many men feel.

This is not to say that men are helpless victims who bear no responsibility for these problems. Indeed, these statistics are the product of a society largely run by men. But it does indicate that men are suffering in a fundamental way. They are experiencing, according to Herb Goldberg in *The Hazards of Being Male,* the "costs of gender privilege." In many ways, men have victimized themselves.

THE UNDERFATHERED SON

It's one thing to talk abstractly about the overall effects of industry in our culture, but it's quite another to experience these effects at the personal level, in the culture of our families. In this century, home has been the place where passivity has taken root in millions of men.

Psychologists agree that in order for a person to grow into a whole and healthy individual, he must undergo the process of emotionally bonding with and separating from both of his parents. When the men of the 1800s left their farms and home-based trades for jobs in the factories, suddenly a generation of sons—and every generation since—was deprived of the ongoing physical presence of the father. Of course daughters experienced this loss too and have had their share of resulting problems. But they still had their mother to learn femininity from. The father's departure is especially devastating to the son, who needs his father's presence in order to bond with him and learn what it means to be a man.

When a son spends hours each day standing next to his father—working, relaxing, facing problems, making decisions, playing—he picks up a great deal of the stuff of masculinity, stuff that can't be learned from a book or from his mother. Unfortunately, very few men in recent history have had that kind of positive experience with their fathers. More than likely, a son got up just in time (if he was lucky) to see his father off to work. He didn't really know exactly what kind of work his father did, other than the name of a company or the kind of product. And he rarely if ever saw his father at work, on the job, and experienced daily life along with him. When his father arrived home at the end of the day, exhausted and often irritated, the son wanted to be with him, but somehow knew he had to keep his distance.

Perhaps no song in recent times has captured the dynamics of the absent father and the longing son like the ballad "Cat's in the Cradle" by Harry Chapin, with its haunting refrain:

> *When you coming home, Dad, I don't know when*
> *But we'll get together then*
> *You know we'll have a good time then.*[4]

An episode of the TV series *The Wonder Years* also depicts this gap between father and son, and the son's yearning to understand something of a man's world. The show chronicles the life and times of the Arnold family, who live in a postwar prefab suburb in the late 1960s, as seen through the eyes of its preteen son, Kevin. Every day Kevin watches his father leave for the office in the morning and storm into the house angrily at night. It occurs to him that he has no idea what his father does during the day or what might be causing the tension and anger he sees each night. He decides to ask his dad if he could go to work with him sometime. At first Dad gives him a gruff rebuff, but after a gentle prod from Kevin's mother, he agrees.

A few days later Kevin, dressed in a suit, accompanies his father to the office. Though his dad's job consists mainly of filling out forms and talking on the phone (he's an inventory control manager), Kevin is still mesmerized by the power and authority he seems to wield. He watches his father issue orders, delegate responsibility, answer people's questions, and solve problems, and he feels his chest swelling with pride in his dad as the day progresses. *If this is what working is like,* he says to himself, *maybe it's not so bad. Maybe I'll even follow in my dad's footsteps someday.*

As five o'clock approaches and they prepare to leave, however, his dad's boss bursts into the office. In Kevin's presence, he proceeds to ream out Kevin's father in a cruel and insulting manner for a problem he was not responsible for. Kevin could see the anger, humiliation, and shame on his father's face, but his father didn't fight with the boss, because in those days challenging the boss could mean losing one's job.

The scene then changes back to the Arnolds' kitchen, where the rest of the family is waiting at the dinner table for Kevin and his father to return from work. There is the screech of tires pulling into the driveway and the wham of the car door. Kevin's father storms through the kitchen door as usual, throws down his briefcase in disgust, and heads for the evening paper without a word. A moment later, Kevin angrily charges in exactly as his father did and slams the door behind him. Like father, like son.

That final scene dramatizes the dilemma that so many men have had to face in this mechanized age: Our fathers (and most likely their fathers) were forced out of their homes and into impersonal jobs they didn't want, with bureaucratic structures that stifled creativity and a sense of individual worth. They felt like mere cogs on the wheels of Progress, with very few choices in the kind of life and work they could pursue. They felt powerless and angry at the forces that seemed to be controlling their lives. And since they were never taught how to deal with that anger and powerlessness, they unknowingly passed it on to their sons.

I recall the image of my father coming home from work—late most of the time, because insurance salespeople rarely keep a fixed 9-to-5 schedule. When he didn't have to work in the evening, he'd be home at 6:30 or so, and we usually waited to have dinner until he arrived. He often seemed uptight and irritable, like he'd been forced to do something against his will. During dinner I'd sometimes ask what he did during the day. His answer was usually the same: "Oh, I had a few meetings, wrote a few letters, made a few phone calls." He didn't say much else. After eating he'd retreat to his recliner chair in the den, where he'd read the paper or catch the TV news, put his head back, and drift off to sleep. My two brothers and I knew to give Dad his space, because he usually didn't have the energy or the patience to deal with us.

"When a father, absent during the day, returns home at six, his children receive only his temperament, and not his teaching," Robert Bly writes in *Iron John*.[5] The children may also fail to connect with the love their father has for them but doesn't know how to express. Kevin Arnold and I and millions of other men experienced more of the angry, hard, and distant sides of our fathers than we did the intimate, teaching sides.

And where did that leave me? Wounded, though I didn't know it at the time. I felt empty, hollow, hungry. I had little sense of what it meant to be a man, and no one to teach me. My peers were for the most part in the same situation as I, and I had no male relatives or other older men nearby to serve as role models. I wanted a deeper relationship with my father, but when I didn't get it, I felt betrayed, suspicious, and resentful, not only of him but of father figures, people in authority, and older men in general. If there was anyone in the world I didn't want to be like, it was my father.

Now keep in mind that my father has never been addicted to alcohol or drugs, has married only once and remained faithful to his wife to this day, has provided his family with a comfortable, upper-middle-class lifestyle, and has tried to live authentically as an evangelical Christian and regular churchgoer. Why should I complain, especially after hearing some of my friends describe the horrific abuse and neglect they suffered from their fathers?

Certainly I'm grateful that Dad had fewer problems to pass on to me than many fathers, but I can't really compare him to anyone else. Only one man in the world is my father, and he met some of my childhood needs and didn't meet others; he helped me in some ways and he hurt me in others. My experience of being helped or hurt is unique, based on my own childhood perceptions. And I believe every man can look back on his early years and identify ways in which he experienced some kind of wound from his father. Indeed, some men I know can't recall anything but wounds. Whatever a man's childhood was like, coming to terms with the wounds he received is essential, because adult passivity stems from childhood wounds.

The unexamined wounds of our father—the wounds not understood or not treated or not healed—get passed on to us, sometimes consciously, sometimes not. The wounds he's received from our techno-society, from our quick-fix culture, from the church, from inflexible institutions, and from his own father—unless he's been able to come to terms with them somehow, to draw upon the inner growth-energy those wounds have created, he will passively transfer those wounds to us, his sons. We've already seen that our father's absence alone has caused a wound. There are many more kinds. Physical or sexual abuse inflicts a deep wound. A father who is unavailable, rageful, shaming, or overly critical causes injury to his son.

In the Monday night men's support group I attend, virtually everyone present—ten to twenty guys each week—had an absent, unavailable, or abusive father. One man was regularly beaten and literally tortured by his father as a way to wrangle money from his mother. This man described horrifying scenes of boiling water poured on him, of being dangled by one foot out of upper-story windows, of having all his hair shaved off and being sent to school, and other atrocities, some of which his mother stopped (by giving in to the father), and some of which she didn't. I can't even imagine the depth of pain this man carries within himself each day.

Others say they grew up with fathers who rarely if ever affirmed them. They always felt they had to do things, to perform, in order to please their fathers and receive their love and blessing. Unfortunately, most of these fathers told them they couldn't do anything right, which caused another kind of wound. "I can only remember one time as a child that my father affirmed me in any way," a man recalled. "He told me he liked a picture of a car that I drew." The man's childhood hunger for approval was so great, and the impact of one lone compliment so strong, that today he sells cars for a living, and continues to draw pictures of cars. But he still struggles with poor self-esteem and wonders if he'll ever amount to anything.

Another man in the group had a father who moved away for the first nine years of his life to start a business. When he finally did return, he had made lots of money and showered the children with gifts and sports opportunities. But the most important thing—his father's presence and interest— was still missing:

> [My dad] kept buying me things, and every summer I went away to another camp, always an athletic camp. I went to football camp, I went to tennis camp, I went to every kind of camp, every summer of my life. I had this feeling that something was up, because I had never had any real intimacy with my dad. I remember thinking, "Why do I always have to go to camp?" Once I found myself standing alone in the middle of Logan airport in Boston, wondering, "What am I doing here?" I was getting all this from my dad and I felt like I had to pay him back. I remember always trying to excel, especially in athletics.

On many occasions during my childhood, I would help my father with carpentry projects around the house. Whenever I made a mistake such as bending a nail or dropping a tool, Dad would blow up at me in anger. "I'm sorry!" I'd protest. And he'd retort, "You're not sorry, you're careless!" I think that phrase, which he repeated over the years, amounted to a wound in my psyche. I now know that he wasn't trying to wound me, but at the time I had no defense. Even today I struggle with inner voices that accuse me of carelessness or laziness.

Sometimes the wound of a father's absence comes through death, as another man in the group explains:

> My father died when I was seven, and I felt a tremendous loss. Four years later, when my childhood sweetheart was breaking up with me, I said, "Why? Is it because my father's dead?" I felt so inferior. Another time an art teacher [who didn't know my father had died] said to me, "If you don't quit fooling around in class, I'm going to have your father come to school," and I just burst into tears. So I feel like I've always been looking for that male identity that I never got from my father. I tried to pose as being a tough guy, and I played football and lifted weights, and I swaggered, and I tried to seduce every woman in sight, but on the inside I basically felt cowardly. Today, I'm afraid of angry people, I'm afraid of getting into conflict, and I back down, and then I feel so shamed. I'm not able to assert myself when I'd like to. I've just never taken responsibility for my life. I've always thought that whenever I got in a pinch, that somebody would step in and pick up the tab for me, or somebody would take care of me.

How do wounds such as these cause a man to become passive? Usually by causing him to click into certain kinds of behavior (such as those described in the previous chapter) whenever his life touches on the area in which the wound occurred. Most of the time, the man who has not faced his father's wounds either repeats his father's wounding behavior or overcompensates by doing the opposite. A man whose father was angry all the time may find that he too easily explodes in anger, or else he may close down his feelings altogether. In either case, he's usually not making a conscious choice; his response is nearly automatic, as if a switch had been flipped.

I received one of my wounds in the area of self-esteem. The messages I heard led me to believe that I was only acceptable to my father when I performed according to his standards, without making a mistake. In my mind, "You're not sorry—you're careless" meant that mistakes were bad, and that if I made a mistake, I was bad. This early verdict attached itself to me as I grew older, so that deep down, even I believed I was bad or careless or not good enough in whatever I did. New projects or challenges immediately prompted the unarticulated question, "How can I do this perfectly, without making a mistake?" Then, afraid that I'd fall short of perfection and therefore be worthless as a person, I'd click into a pattern of procrastination and paralysis. It's the click that makes it passive: The behavior happens automatically, robotically, as if I had no choice, as if I had at some point abdicated responsibility for my actions, which is exactly what I have done. And it began with the father wound.

THE OVERMOTHERED SON

From kindergarten through at least junior high, every day when I came home from school, my mother was waiting for me. I'd give her a big hug, then plop down at the kitchen table for some cookies and milk, or else I'd pour myself a bowl of Frosted Flakes. While she sat across from me, listening intently, I proceeded to give her an hour-by-hour breakdown of what happened at school that day—quizzes or tests I took, fun or interesting activities, kids I hung around with, kids who picked on me. I felt very cared about, very paid attention to. Usually I had papers or art to show her, and she'd nod approvingly, since I tended to get good grades. Fifteen or twenty minutes later I'd scamper back out the door to play ball with the other neighborhood kids.

Though I look back on those afternoons with a certain fondness, I also see how they set up an unhealthy precedent in our household. I learned, along with my two younger brothers, that Mom was the one to tell everything to, the one to confide in. After all, she was always around, always willing to drop everything and listen if I needed to talk. Dad, on the other hand, came home later on, and he seemed too tense and tired to hear about every minute of my day. So as things came up in my life—questions, problems, struggles—I learned to save them for Mom. Over the years I came to depend heavily on her rather than my father to "be there" for me, to help me sort things out, to provide support. And she always seemed to rise to the occasion.

I see now that I was an overmothered son. At its simplest, overmothering means that the amount of time the mother devotes to the son is much greater—often hugely disproportionate—to the time the father spends with the son. If sons only rarely bonded with their fathers, they bonded too tightly to their mothers. It's a natural consequence of the father's exodus to the factories and offices. The mother simply inherited sole responsibility for the children during the day. And since she traditionally stayed home for the first hundred years after the Industrial Revolution began, she ended up being the son's primary source of information—verbal and nonverbal—about what it means to grow up and be a man. The mother's strong presence often skewed the son's view of manhood, making it much more difficult for him to separate emotionally from her as he grew older.

In many families, the tradition continues to this day, and sons still spend much more time with their mothers than their fathers, though the increase in working mothers has reduced the proportion somewhat. (It will be interesting to see how these sons are affected by the shift as they become adults.) But the large majority of men reading this book, I suspect, grew up almost exclusively under the care and tutelage of their mothers. Even if our mothers gave us a reasonably healthy upbringing, it was still primarily a feminine upbringing, which included a feminine view of the world, a feminine view of our fathers, and a feminine view of masculinity. Her view is not necessarily wrong, but it is only a partial view; and if we remain overly connected to our mothers, we make her view the dominant one in our own adult male lives.

So far I'm assuming that the state of the home is basically positive or neutral. How does the mother's view affect sons if the father is absent, alcoholic, abusive, or away at work all the time? One way or another, her attempts to compensate for the missing father will bind the sons more closely to her (and women in general). Further, the sons are likely to pick up on her frustration or anger at the father (or men in general). According to one man in this situation, the effect on him was terribly damaging:

> My father and I never got along because he didn't bother with me and I didn't bother with him. He never took me aside and showed me how to do things around the house. My mother ran the place, and she took care of everything, and I just continued along in life. She greatly influenced my mental attitude toward men, which was lousy. When I reached the age of eighteen, instead of getting my head together and saying, "Well, fine, this is what she says, but it doesn't make sense," I just blindly believed it. When I got married, I figured my wife should take care of everything; I just sat back and didn't worry about it. As a result, my wife and I have fought for thirty out of the thirty-two years we've been married. I'm just starting to realize that what I've been doing is wrong; it hasn't been helping me or my wife or the marriage. Now I'm trying to rectify it the best I can.

Here we see a pattern that has ensnared millions of men in passivity during this century: The father is absent, abusive, or unavailable, alienating the son and placing too heavy a burden on the mother. The mother tries to fill the void left by the father, but she cannot avoid conveying her resentment to the son. The son, moved by his mother's pain, takes her side and turns against his father (and older men in general). When he reaches adulthood, he unconsciously looks for someone just like his mother to marry, and ends up playing the same passive role he played as a boy.

It's important to note here that I'm not talking about blaming mothers (or fathers) for this problem. Blame is not the issue; besides, if I tried to blame mothers, they could easily say that it started with the father's absence. And then the fathers could blame the factories, and so on. What I'm trying to show is a general pattern that began with the Industrial Revolution and involved fathers and mothers and their sons. Because of the father's absence, the son was never able to bond with him; and because of the mother's overpresence, the son was never able to separate from her. Just as the father's exit from the household creates a wound in the sons, so does the mother's overinvolvement. Both make it extremely difficult for sons to grow into mature, independent adult men.

A too-present mother may, consciously or unconsciously, inflict other wounds on her son besides that of male resentment. Violating her son's personal boundaries through overprotection, overintrusiveness, or inappropriate sharing of one's personal life can cause a wound. It is not unusual for a mother to use her son to fill her own unmet needs. If the father is absent for the son, he's also likely to be absent for his wife. Without even realizing it, a mother may foster unhealthy affection with her son, not to show appropriate motherly love and care, but rather to meet her own need for intimacy. Whenever this happens, no matter how subtly, it wounds the son by binding him too tightly to his mother, severely crippling his ability to separate from her emotionally.

Gavin, a regular in the Monday men's group, described how his mother went so far as to state her need directly in his presence:

> I became aware very early on that my father was not satisfying my mother's romantic needs. Once she even said to my father, right in front of me, "Why don't you touch me the way Gavin does?"

That simple statement by his mother must have inflicted a deep wound on Gavin. Immediately he knew he was special to her, that he had a closer connection to her than his own father did, perhaps even a sexual connection. He saw his father as the bad guy, and his mother as the poor oppressed one. It's as if the mother has cast a spell on the son. Suddenly things get muddied, and boundaries are blurred. The lines between the mother's relationship to the father and to the son seem to fade, and the gap between son and father widens. The son is only a kid, but he's being asked (usually nonverbally) to meet an adult woman's needs. And a kid doesn't know what's really going on—he doesn't know how to say, "Hey look, Mom, I can't be your substitute husband!" So he has little choice but to run into his mother's arms.

Some mental health professionals have gone so far as to say this amounts to a form of covert incest on the part of the mother. At the very least, it is an unspoken alliance, with mother and son on one side and the father on the other. There is a knowing quality about it: The message the mother communicates to the son is something like, "Don't worry, everything will be all right. You can always come to me. I'll always be there for you, even if your father won't." The very moment a boy accepts that message—and he has no choice but to accept it because if he didn't, he'd have nobody—that very moment, he falls into a trance. From then on, he remains under his mother's spell. By now he's been even more alienated from the world of his father and of men; all he can feel is her feelings and her needs. But what about his own? He has no idea; his feelings have been swallowed up in his mother's. When he becomes an adult, he still won't have any idea. Instead of learning to become a separate individual, with his own feelings and needs, he learns to look up to his mother, then to his wife, and then to women in general to find out what they are feeling. And in some vague, mushy way, he expects them to know his needs and be there for him.

Listen to another man describe how his life turned out after growing up in this kind of setting:

> I was raised by my mother and my two [much older] sisters. Not only did they raise me and have all the parental influence on me, but on top of that, my father was an alcoholic. As a result of his acting out, my sisters and mother had a very low opinion of him and they ingrained that in me. So I grew up looking to women as the leaders, the rulers, the ones who had all the answers, the ones who had everything I needed. And I viewed men as not having anything of value. I carried that perception through four marriages. In three of them, the women were exactly like my mother. I have nobody to blame but myself [for choosing them]. When I got into relationships with those women, and with others in-between, I would stop being me and let them take over, just like I did when I was a little boy.

The kind of overmothering I've outlined here is a sure-fire formula for passivity because it numbs men to their own feelings and instead causes them to focus completely on the feelings of the mother and, later, of other women. Further, overmothering leads men to passively expect their mothers and wives to step in and meet their needs.

Female traits can and should be encouraged in men. So many men are afraid to show tenderness and fear and hurt and other emotions that women can express more easily. Men need to be willing to nurture the female side of themselves, and mothers can be helpful in this process. But when it comes to a man's masculine traits, which include his perception of fatherhood and of mature manhood, these cannot be obtained through the mother, no matter how hard she tries or how pure her motives are. Unless a mother can recognize the limits of her ability to develop her son's manhood and stay on her side of the line, she'll end up with a passive man every time.

The dilemma of men who are overly connected to their mothers is nothing new. Though the Industrial Revolution exacerbated the problem, it didn't start it. In the Bible, Jacob was much closer to his mother, Rebekah, than to his father, Isaac (Genesis 25:28). When the time came for the oldest son, Esau, to receive Isaac's official blessing, Rebekah took Jacob into her confidence and conspired with him to deceive Isaac (Genesis 27). Though the story does not specifically state that Jacob received a mother-wound at this point, it's quite clear in the chapters that follow that Jacob had much difficulty in his relationships with women and tended to play the passive role.

Perhaps the mother-son-father conflict has been going on since the dawn of humanity. Maybe it even occurs at the genetic level, since the mother feels the physical bond of carrying and giving birth to the boy, while the father is more detached from the process. And once the son is born, he probably feels a closer biological bond with his mother as well (assuming he received adequate love and care from her).

Many psychologists believe that the son's struggle to bond with and separate from his mother takes place on a much larger scale in the male psyche, as if it were an inner drama. Robert A. Johnson (along with other followers of Carl Jung) writes of the "mother complex," the part of a man that both wants the world to be his mother and is terrified of being swallowed up if that were to happen. Johnson says that the mother complex is

> the greatest stumbling block that exists in a man's psychology. Almost no man will admit it, which means that he is probably totally eaten up by it. But as a man grows, he has a chance to make a better relationship with his mother complex.[6]

To become a mature, independent man, Johnson and others argue, a man must come to terms with the mother at two levels: with his real mother, and with his inner mother complex. Though the two may have some overlapping traits, they are not the same and should be kept distinct. Unless the grown son resolves his mother issues at both levels, he may be doomed to a life of passivity. Carl Jung explains what can happen:

> The unsatisfied longing of the son for life and world ought to be taken seriously. There is in him a desire to touch reality, to embrace the earth and fructify the field of the world. But he makes no more than a series of fitful starts, for his initiative as well as his staying power are crippled by the secret memory that the world and happiness may be had as a gift—from the mother. The fragment of the world which he, like every man, must encounter again and again is never quite the right one, since it does not fall into his lap, does not meet him half way, but remains resistant, has to be conquered, and submits only to force. It makes demands of the masculinity of a man, on his ardor, above all on his courage and resolution when it comes to throwing his whole being into the scales. For this he would need . . . [to be] capable of forgetting his mother and undergoing the pain of relinquishing the first love of his life. The mother, foreseeing this danger, has carefully inculcated into him the virtues of faithfulness, devotion, loyalty, so as to protect him from the moral disruption which is the risk of every life adventure. He has learnt these lessons only too well, and remains true to his mother.[7]

Note the references to passivity, such as "gift from the mother," "fall into his lap," and "meet him halfway." But also note the positive masculine traits that can develop if the man does resolve his inner and outer mother issues: "initiative," "staying power," "ardor," "courage," "resolution," "throwing his whole being into the scales." These are the traits that I and so many other passive men want to develop more of.

PASSIVE ON THE LEFT, PASSIVE ON THE RIGHT

So far in this discussion on the roots of male passivity, I have explored the effects of industry and technology on our culture in general, and how these sweeping changes have created generations of men who are underfathered and overmothered. There are two more factors in recent society that have contributed to the rise in male passivity—one coming from the political left, and one from the right. I'd like to examine these briefly before closing this chapter.

On the left are some of the side-effects of the feminist movement, which generally had a positive impact on the men of North America. Feminism helped many of them to cast off some of the longstanding destructive traits of pseudo-masculinity such as power mongering, dominating women, and hiding emotion. Men began to accept women more as equals and to acknowledge and express their own feminine side. But rather than balance the feminine and the masculine sides, many men (usually unconsciously) embraced the feminine at the *expense of* their masculine side.

Part of the impetus for this trend came from a small but vocal group of radical feminists (as opposed to mainstream "sensible feminists") who believed that maleness in itself (as opposed to a patriarchal system) was somehow the cause of most of the world's injustices. These extremists took male/female equality one step too far by preaching that men and women are not only equal, but are the *same*, and that there are no differences between them other than the reproductive system. Though not a predominant force, they created just enough insecurity among American men that many of them felt guilty about being a man, and assumed that they had to atone for their sex's centuries of oppressing women by giving up their masculinity altogether.

Men have much to be grateful for in the feminist movement. But those men who have given in to feminist fringe elements who favor giving up the masculine side, or worse, apologizing for being a man, will find themselves hopelessly trapped with no sense of identity. Nevertheless, these fringe groups have contributed to male passivity.

So much for the left. On the right, which includes political conservatives and many evangelical Christians, I see a well-intentioned moral agenda with a few confusing aspects, ones that unwittingly foster passivity in boys and men. Many Christians champion "family values," for instance, without really stopping to ask what makes them family values. One such "value" I've heard states that the husband should be the family breadwinner, and the wife should stay home with the children. But in light of the devastating impact of absent fathers on the home, does it really enhance and strengthen the family to have the father work long hours and render himself unavailable (especially) to his son? I realize that economic realities come into play here, but a blanket endorsement of such a "value" often deprives sons of the most important model they need to become mature men.

Boys in today's society need all the help they can get to develop a clear sense of their male identity. They desperately need their fathers and other men to serve as role models. And yet, in North America today, boys (and girls) receive virtually constant care and training by women for the first eighteen years of their lives—at home with their mothers, in daycare centers run by women, in schools with mostly women teachers, even in Sunday schools led predominantly by women. No wonder these boys get hooked into unhealthy, passive relationships with women later on. Please understand that I am not trying to disparage women or minimize their value as nurturers and teachers. I'm saying that children need *both* men and women involved in their care and training. And when the world in which they grow up is dominated by women, it's the boys especially who suffer.

There are all kinds of explanations for this dilemma, and I won't go into them here. But I sense a vague sort of complicity on the part of many churches. While they charge into great theological battles to limit the leadership role of women in the church, they allow their women Sunday school teachers to become the primary source of spiritual influence and instruction in their children's lives. Men may hold the official positions in the church, but at the day-to-day personal level, the feminine influence dominates. Again, the boys come up short.

Another way that many Christian families and churches reinforce passivity is by assuming that God will somehow exempt them from the problems of other families. Pastors, missionaries, and church and parachurch workers sometimes believe that because they are pursuing a spiritual ministry, they can work long hours and sacrifice their family time in order to serve God and still expect the children to turn out okay. Unfortunately, there are myriad accounts of pastors' kids and missionaries' kids who rebelled because of a lack of attention from their parents. No matter what beliefs or values a family holds, it takes active, consistent work on the part of both parents to raise healthy children.

Amid all the reasons and explanations for passivity in men, I cannot avoid what may be the most significant cause of all: men's own failure to take responsibility for their lives. For the past few decades, a growing number of men have been looking for some kind of role model for mature manhood, someone who could show them that it was possible to respect women and show one's feelings and be nurturing without having to abandon one's masculinity; that it was possible to be clear, firm, and forthright without being domineering; that it was possible to be equal with women and yet different. But sadly, they found few if any authentic role models. Their own fathers were absent or unavailable, their bosses were still caught up in the old authoritarian system, and their government leaders were either corrupt or too busy fighting the communists.

So instead of looking within themselves and to each other for strength and support, as the women already knew how to do, men again turned to external, superficial means of holding on to the fragments of their selfhood: pursuing successful, lucrative careers, focusing on competition, performance and achievement, acquiring possessions to create a semblance of security. Men have always had the inner power to rise up against difficult odds, but they haven't always exercised the courage. Jung writes:

> It is often tragic to see how blatantly a man bungles his own life and the lives of others yet remains totally incapable of seeing how much the whole tragedy originates in himself, and how he continually feeds it and keeps it going. Not consciously, of course—for consciously he is engaged in bewailing and cursing a faithless world that recedes further and further into the distance. Rather, it is an unconscious factor which spins the illusions that veil his world.[8]

I've attempted here to explore some of these unconscious factors that lead to passivity in men. Now it's time to find out how some passive men have begun to take responsibility and make some changes in their lives.

Three

A Movement Among Men

Men go crazy in congregations
But they only get better
One by one
One by one . . .

— *Sting*

In the past few years news of a growing "men's movement" has hit the covers of *Time, Newsweek,* and *Esquire,* and reached television's PBS specials and ABC's *20/20,* among others. Jokes have flourished about male bonding and about naked men running around the forests and beating drums on "wildman weekends." Prime-time TV sitcoms such as *Murphy Brown, Designing Women,* and *Cheers* have focused entire episodes on the men's movement. In the fall of 1991 the sitcom *Home Improvement* popped up about a man trying to get in touch with his masculinity. To everyone's surprise, the show landed in the top ten for the season. Most of the programs ridiculed the movement, but according to one writer who has followed men's issues, "When they're making jokes, they're taking you seriously."[1] Maybe so, but popular media coverage has given the general public an extremely distorted picture of the men's movement. Why? Sensationalism sells papers and increases viewers. Focusing on the extreme makes it easy to criticize and ridicule while ignoring the movement's deeper undercurrents.[2]

In the Christian community, responses vary. Many men reject the movement outright as a new-age affront to Christian values. Others resonate with issues such as passivity and the need to work on their father relationships, but they hunger for a more Christian context to explore these issues.

What is the so-called men's movement? Is it a primitive brotherhood of guys who wished they'd taken drum lessons as a kid? Is it merely another new-age self-help phenomenon? An attempt to return to the old male stereotypes of power and domination? Does it have a national organization and structure, or a toll-free number such as 1-800-REAL-MEN? Is there any value in it? Does it have anything to say to the passive man?

Before I explain how the movement relates to issues of male passivity, I'd like to give some recent historical background in this chapter. For the most part, today's men's movement has arisen out of two other rapidly growing movements of the past two decades: feminism and recovery.

FEMINISM

As our American techno-culture zoomed through the 1960s and 1970s, with power, performance, competition, and efficiency controlling so many men's lives, something had to give. Men were getting to the point where they couldn't go on living the dead-end, deny-who-you-are-and-submit-to-the-organization lifestyle. They needed somewhere to turn, someone to help them find their selves again.

At first many of them turned to women. The rise of the women's movement in the 1960s and 1970s struck a chord with a sizable segment of the men's population, young men in particular. Prompted by the women's call for equal rights in the workplace and the home, these men began to question and rebel against the patriarchal systems based on power and oppression. The father, and everything that seemed to function as an extension of the father—business, higher education, government and the military, organized religion, and authority in general—came under fire. Meanwhile, the mother and her extensions—oppressed women, mother earth, and so on—were praised and championed.

Much of this rebellion was right and necessary, for so many of our institutions were (and still are) power-oriented and male-dominated, at the expense of women, minorities, and the poor. Women benefited greatly by standing up to their male oppressors and fighting for change (though there's still a long way to go), and by giving themselves the freedom to pursue the kind of life they wanted. Men, too, benefited: As they began to make more room for women in the workplace, government, and the church, they also began to pay attention to the feminine side of themselves. Many men gave themselves permission to be vulnerable and express emotions, participate more fully in nurturing and rearing children, be pacifists, and follow a give-and-take approach to decision-making. This development was of vital importance because it began to correct some of the inner imbalances brought on by the Industrial Revolution and centuries of oppressing women. But as for helping men reclaim their deeper, fuller masculine identity, it was only a first step.

Unfortunately, a large percentage of the men who adopted feminist values stopped right there, thinking they had found the missing link to their identity. What they actually did, however, was to reject their raw and undeveloped masculine side altogether and adopt a feminine view of the world and a feminine view of their own male identity. More and more men, myself included, would subconsciously say to themselves, "Who do women [or my wife, my girlfriend, or my mother] want me to be? Okay, then that's who I'll be." Rather than look inward to find their identity, most of these feminist men looked outward, to the world of women. Passivity beckoned.

Church denominations responded in a variety of ways to the feminist movement. Some rushed to embrace changes that permitted women to serve in leadership positions and even as ministers and priests. Others resorted to halfway measures that gave women a little more official involvement in church government. More conservative denominations were either galvanized against feminist values or else fought bitter battles over women's roles in church. Many are still fighting. But amid all the upheaval, whether out of agreement or disagreement with feminism, many men in the church began to "soften" too. When this softening occurred as a way of relinquishing old patterns of male domination, it was good. But many softened out of insecurity, feeling threatened by women, reacting on the outside without knowing what was happening on the inside. Often these men would become wishy-washy, using spiritual euphemisms such as "Christlikeness" or "meekness" or "waiting upon the Lord" to justify their indecisiveness or passivity. One woman I know told of getting a call from her boyfriend, who without warning announced to her that he had "lost his peace" about their relationship. She later learned that the man's parents had disapproved of her; he had failed to be honest either with them or with her.

Jesuit priest and professor Patrick M. Arnold put it bluntly: "Newly neutered Christianity is beginning to produce a generation of men with no 'wildness' and no 'fight' in them, a blow-dried, Gucci-shoed and sun-tanned lot whose primary moral achievement is 'being nice.'"[3]

Still, for many of these softer men, things seemed to go well for a while. They tended to pair up with stronger women who enjoyed their newfound freedom and power. The women liked a man who listened to their needs, gave them the freedom to pursue a career, and helped with domestic duties. And the men felt less restricted to the automatic, age-old roles of Provider and Protector. They enjoyed knowing that they were pleasing their wives and helping them achieve a fuller life. But before long it became clear that something wasn't working. Wives became frustrated because it seemed their husbands were taking little or no initiative of their own, not just in helping around the house, but in expressing and following their own inner desires. These men seemed to have no identity of their own; all they did was stand around and wait for their wives or partners to take the lead.

Sadly, most of these men didn't even know they needed to find inner strength and resolve, and if they had, they have no idea where to start looking. Frustration and confusion quickly set in. As my first marriage began to crumble, I remember saying, "Good grief—what else can I do? I'm pitching in a lot more around the house, I've given her a night out each week, I've encouraged her get her own job and explore her own career options. What more does she want?"

I don't really know all of what was going on in my first wife's head at that time. Apart from her dissatisfaction with me, she was dealing with plenty of her own problems and issues; the whole situation was much more complex than I'm describing here. But as I look back on who I was in the midst of that decaying marriage, I see that I indeed fit the "soft male" pattern Bly discusses.[4] I never bothered to look inside myself to ask what I wanted or needed; all I could do was obsess about how to meet her needs, fix her problems, make her happy. And I believe many other men over the past twenty years have experienced something similar. More and more of these men stood by and watched in despair as their marriages fell apart. Often, as in my case, the wives were the ones to leave or to initiate the divorce, which only made the men feel worse about themselves.

In short, feminism was an important first step for men, but not the only step they needed to reclaim their male identity. Those who felt feminism was The Answer usually ended up becoming nice, passive men, following the lead of women, trying to perform for them and please them, trying to prove that men were no longer the oppressors they used to be. Even the men who pooh-poohed the women's movement found themselves on the defensive: They still had to make superficial changes to create the impression that they were fair to women, which meant they too were operating by an external rather than an internal standard. In either case, men remained unfulfilled and unsure of themselves as men. Something additional was needed to help them find their identity.

RECOVERY

In the 1970s and 1980s, another movement began to gather momentum. Though Alcoholics Anonymous meetings had been taking place around the country for forty years, the general public began to realize for the first time that the Twelve Steps of AA offered help and hope not only to alcoholics, but to people struggling with any kind of addiction—drugs, cigarettes, food, gambling, and more. And with the dramatic rise of drug and alcohol use during the turbulent 1960s and early 1970s, North American society offered up a large crop of addicted baby-boomers, the majority of whom were men.

Some of these men had used drugs to achieve a higher, more enlightened consciousness; that is, they mistakenly believed drugs would help them get in touch with deeper, spiritual parts of themselves. Others felt they needed drugs and alcohol to cope with a culture that was steadily increasing the pressure on men to perform and be successful. Still others simply wanted to party. Whatever the case, they began to realize after a few years that their substances and habits had become addictions and that their life and health were being sapped away rather than enhanced. Before long more and more men were turning to Alcoholics Anonymous, Narcotics Anonymous, Gamblers Anonymous, and so on, to find recovery from their addictions. (Millions of women attended as well, and I don't want to detract one bit from the value of these Twelve-Step groups to them; I'm simply zeroing in on how men were prepared for the birth of their own movement.)

What did the recovery movement do for men? First, it gave them a place to share their feelings and seek support from other men, both in regular Twelve-Step meetings and one on one. (Even though many groups included both men and women, sharing in the presence of other men was still new for this fresh crop.) Men who took the program seriously usually worked with a sponsor, another man who had remained substance-free in the program for some time. If both sponsor and sponsee were earnestly seeking to improve their lives and remain sober, it was impossible for them to be superficial with each other. More and more, men were entrusting themselves to the care of other men—not to have someone else fix their problems, but to have support while they solved their own.

Second, the Twelve-Step groups were spiritual in nature. They directed men to give up trying to control their own lives and instead allow God (or a "Higher Power") to guide them. The Steps encouraged men to look inward, to search their own hearts, identify their own character defects, seek forgiveness, make amends, pray and meditate, and spread the news of their spiritual awakening to others. The movement struck a balance between yielding oneself to God and also taking responsibility for one's life—an important theme for the men's movement later on.

As these support groups increased in number, important discoveries were made that attracted still more people. The next wave of the recovery movement hit with the wider public's recognition that not only addicts needed support, but their spouses and children, even their grown children. Al-Anon and Alateen (Twelve-Step groups for spouses, partners, and teenage children of alcoholics) had been operating for some years, but it was not until books appeared by John Bradshaw (*Bradshaw on: The Family* and *Healing the Shame that Binds You*) and Janet G. Woititz (*Adult Children of Alcoholics* and *Struggle for Intimacy*) that large numbers of hurting men and women came out of the woodwork and sought help. Thousands flocked to Bradshaw's seminars and watched his PBS television series, and thousands more formed Adult Children of Alcoholics (ACOA) groups around the country. Book sales soared into the millions. It only made sense that this wave could be larger than that of addicts, since one alcoholic could affect his spouse and all his children, and—if they didn't get help—all his grandchildren as well.

The most recent wave in the recovery movement promised to be larger yet. The word *codependent* had been coined in the late 1970s to refer to the overaffected spouse/partner of an alcoholic, but by 1987, with the publication of *Codependent No More* by Melody Beattie, the term had taken on a much broader meaning, one that had implications for tens of millions of people. Beattie defined the codependent as "one who has let another person's behavior affect him or her, and who is obsessed with controlling that person's behavior."[5] Her ideas rang true for the masses, and the book thrived on the best-seller list for more than two years, spawning yet another branch of the Twelve-Step movement, Codependents Anonymous (CoDA). Recovery was now reaching into mainstream America, to people who may not have had any direct involvement with chemical dependency, but who were nevertheless struggling with unhealthy relationships, compulsive behavior, and a lack of power in their lives. Vast numbers of these people, of course, were men.

In Christian circles, people were suspicious of recovery concepts at first because they felt addicts and codependents were denying responsibility for their problems and looking for help outside of Christ. But they couldn't deny that people in their own congregations were finding healing through Twelve-Step programs. Slowly churches began to see the essentially spiritual nature of the Twelve Steps and their consistency with biblical principles. By substituting "God" or "Jesus Christ" for the "Higher Power," they realized that the Twelve Steps could also be a powerful instrument for healing among Christians with addictive or compulsive behaviors. More and more Twelve-Step groups sprang up in evangelical churches (they had already been meeting in mainline churches for many years), and publishers began to release recovery guides with an explicitly Christian foundation.

Many participants in the various AA, ACOA, and CoDA groups found themselves looking back to their childhood to see how abuse, abandonment, neglect, or overinvolvement by one or both parents created a dysfunctional family system. Again and again, across the sexes, even across religious backgrounds, the pattern emerged of the father who was absent, abusive, or unavailable, and the mother who in some way tried to compensate for the father's absence.[6] As I've shown in the previous chapter, underfathering and overmothering damages all the children in some way, but it inflicts a deeper wound on boys—a wound that, if not healed, can lead adult men to become compulsive, addictive, and passive.

To sum up, the recovery movement stirred the souls of men by encouraging them to share feelings with each other, to take responsibility for themselves, to seek divine empowerment, and to look inward rather than outward for strength. It also showed them how the wounds of one's family system can show up later as addictions and codependent adult relationships. All of these emphases would figure prominently in the men's movement to come.

As men in Twelve-Step programs came to realize they had similar backgrounds and recovery needs, some of them began to meet on their own to share and support each other. These small groups, which formed throughout the country during the 1980s, became a significant part of the budding men's movement. Something was still missing, however. Even after men curbed their addictions and other destructive behaviors, they still didn't know who they were as men or how to go about reclaiming their male identity. They needed more guidance, a few good role models, and a public forum for them to explore their issues.

TAKING RESPONSIBILITY

If there is such a thing as a national men's movement, many would say it began in early 1990 with Bill Moyers's televised PBS interview with poet Robert Bly, entitled *A Gathering of Men*. Actually, Bly did not start the movement, nor is he the only one or the first one to proclaim the need for profound change in today's men. The movement had begun a decade or two earlier in grassroots fashion, mainly as a positive response to feminism. Support groups, organizations, and newsletters sprang up to assist men in a variety of areas—divorce recovery, fathers' rights, chemical dependency, sex addiction, stress relief, group psychotherapy, new-age spirituality, gay rights, support for people with AIDS, help for ex-offenders, ex-wifebeaters, and many others. Most of these groups had no formal affiliation with each other, and still do not, but the unique approach and enormous popularity of Bly's teaching in the PBS special and his book *Iron John* energized them with a common purpose: to help men take responsibility for their lives.

Because there are so many different branches of men's groups and organizations, Bly prefers to call the upsurge of interest in men's issues "a movement among men" rather than the "men's movement," which implies more of a unified body with a central structure. At this writing, no such unity or structure exists.[7] Meanwhile, local men's centers have opened in many metropolitan areas, offering lectures, classes, support groups, and sometimes psychotherapy. Often these centers sponsor men's seminars led by

Bly and colleagues such as Michael Meade, James Hillman, Robert Moore, and others. Bly has been conducting workshops for men since 1981, and the others maintain active speaking schedules.

Several other writer/speakers have produced books and materials with a similar, complementary approach to male identity: Sam Keen, whose best-seller *Fire in the Belly: On Being a Man* is an artistic, comprehensive, and practical outworking of many ideas Bly touches on; Robert Moore and Douglas Gillette, who use the archetypal imagery of ancient myths to explain important masculine traits in their books *King, Warrior, Magician, Lover* and *The King Within*; John Lee, who mixes Twelve-Step recovery and men's issues with his own experiences in *The Flying Boy, The Flying Boy II,* and *At My Father's Wedding: Reclaiming Your True Masculinity;* and Robert A. Johnson, a Jungian analyst, in his books *HE, SHE,* and *Transformation: Understanding the Three Levels of Masculine Consciousness.*

But it is Bly who has most captivated the American public, men especially. A number of factors account for this. His sage-like appearance—age sixty-five, warm face, wavy white hair—appeals to so many men who have needed a caring father figure or mentor. Onstage at his seminars he tells stories and recites poetry with power, skill, and clarity, often accompanying himself on the bouzouki. His poems, stories, and interpretations go straight for the heart; they are better experienced than studied, though they would also stand up to critical analysis.

Many have called him the patriarch of the men's movement, and many others have elevated him to saint or guru status. Perhaps no one is more surprised by all the attention and adulation than Bly himself, who dislikes the limelight and deeply distrusts the media. He gives few interviews, refuses to appear on talk shows, and loathes being thought of as a pop figure. At the very time that his popularity was reaching its peak, he decided to take the entire year of 1992 off.

These attitudes underscore a certain humility on Bly's part: He is serious about what he does, but he doesn't take himself too seriously. He would never claim that he started the men's movement or that he wants to be its leader. Nor does he agree with everything others in the movement are doing. For instance, he has spoken frequently about men's need to get in touch with the "wild man" inside them, but he now distances himself from the famed "wildman weekends" sensationalized by the press because they have been given too much emphasis.

Another aspect of Bly the man that is both unnerving and refreshing is his refusal to be pegged. He simply will not fit into anyone's psychological, political, or spiritual agenda. Psychologically, Bly relies heavily on Jungian concepts, and he is married to a Jungian analyst, but he also disagrees with the approach of some Jungians. Politically, he tends to lean toward the left, but he has also reprimanded Democrats for their gutlessness. Spiritually, he has been labeled a new-ager by some, and he has appeared in interviews for *New Age* magazine, yet at times he seems to take special pleasure in criticizing new-agers. A self-proclaimed new-ager I know listened to a stack of Bly's audiotapes and afterward told me, "I liked a lot of what he had to say, but he's definitely anti–new age." Regarding Christianity, Bly has spoken out against various aspects of the institutional church, but I have never seen or heard him show disrespect for Christ or for genuine Christian faith. Nor have I heard him publicly affirm the truth of Christianity either.

Bly's unwillingness to be pigeonholed unnerves me because I want him to believe the same things I do. But it also appeals to me because I admire his courage and independence in saying exactly what he feels, without worrying what other people will think of him. Passive men simply cannot bring themselves to feel or speak so freely. I like the fact that he refuses to toe the party line.

The way hero worship operates in this country, as soon as someone becomes a popular public figure, everyone expects him or her to be an authority in all sorts of areas that person knows little or nothing about. Sadly, some stars actually believe they can be such an authority. Bly appears to have no such illusion; I think this is a major reason he chooses not to align himself with specific beliefs, ideologies, or causes. He's not trying to be a theologian or a therapist or a candidate for office.

Robert Bly considers himself first and foremost a poet. He also cares a great deal about the plight of passive, naïve men, and has put his finger on a few key insights that can help millions of them become more responsible and authentic. As I've listened to these insights, I've sensed that the man is on to something, a valuable piece of truth, a truth that even appears to be present in the Bible, but for some reason has been overlooked. Thinking Christians have a phrase that applies to situations like this: "All truth is God's truth." It means that God is the author of all truth, wherever it may be found—in the Bible, in nature, in science, in psychology, in literature. We can recognize and embrace truth in the writings and discoveries of anyone, whether he is a card-carrying Christian or not. We must be discerning, of course; the truth we find in other places cannot contradict explicit biblical truths, or it may not be truth after all. But there is still plenty of room in the world for all kinds of truth in areas the Bible doesn't happen to talk about.

As it turns out, many of Bly's insights have strong spiritual overtones that, if taken one step further, either have clear biblical parallels or can be applied in a Christian context. I'm not trying to baptize this man or say that his teachings are Christian; but I believe his core emphases—

about the stages a man needs to undergo to reach maturity—are true. They seem to be an accurate picture of the way people really are; they have a universal ring of truth. In addition, Christian men especially can benefit from these insights because today's church structures and church pews are packed with passive men who are leading hollow, dreary lives—who desperately need a fresh perspective on what it means to be a man in today's world.

Here are a few of the key themes and emphases of Bly's branch of the men's movement. First, *the movement emphasizes the need for initiation of men from boyhood to manhood.* As I mentioned in the previous chapter, a person needs to bond with and separate from both parents emotionally in order to become a mature adult. Primitive cultures appear to have known this instinctively, because they designed special ceremonies to bring about the separation and to celebrate it, usually when the child reached puberty. These ancient initiation rites were always religious and, in addition to effecting the separation of the boy from his mother, involved the older men passing on the sacred history and spiritual truth of that culture. We still carry on many rituals today, such as Fourth of July parades, graduation ceremonies, church liturgies, baptisms, weddings, and funerals. For some, these are charged with meaning, but for most of us, they often end up as obligatory formalities that we must endure. It may be meaningful, of course, to be together with one's family and friends, but as for the actual ceremony, it usually feels dry, repetitious, devoid of spiritual power.

Positive initiation rituals have virtually disappeared from North America today, at a time when they are badly needed. Twentieth-century men are not completing the separation process from their parents, nor are they plugging themselves into a relationship with God, as the ancient ceremonies helped to bring about. They usually bond with their mothers quite early, but have a hard time making a clean emotional break later; and if they ever bond with their fathers, it's not until three, four, or five decades have passed, and then they still need to separate from them afterward. However far they get in the process before stalling, they have little real contact with God or the spiritual realm.

Furthermore, today's society has snuffed out the old ways of helping boys through the transition to manhood. The fathers aren't around like they used to be, and uncles or grandfathers who might be able to help live in some other state. Besides, few if any of them made the transition either. So generations of boys are becoming adults physically, but remaining emotionally stuck in boyhood. And all we're left with are negative, destructive rites such as those practiced by gangs or college fraternities. Robert Bly and others are saying that men need to work at completing their own initiation process, not only for their own growth but in order to help other boys and young men take the leap into the mature masculine world. (Women too need to go through these transitions and need their own separate rituals.)

Bly's own book about men, *Iron John,* is based on a Grimm fairy tale compiled in the early 1800s but originating thousands of years earlier. It is the story of a boy's journey to adulthood and his apprenticeship to Iron John, a wild man who had been discovered at the bottom of a swamp. As Bly retells the various stages and trials the boy must face along the way, he pauses to explain how they parallel many ancient initiation rites, and further, how they mirror the passages men need to go through today.

Second, *the movement encourages men to engage in soul-tending.* In today's society, men have been told to work hard, produce, perform, be efficient. Busyness and long hours are praised: "If you want to be sure something gets done, ask a busy person," the saying goes. But when can a

man find time to reflect on who he is, to nurture the inner
life of his soul? Sam Keen writes:

> Men, in our culture, have carried a special burden of
> unconsciousness, or ignorance of the self. The unexam-
> ined life has been worth quite a lot in economic terms. It
> has enabled us to increase the gross national product
> yearly. It may not be necessary to be a compulsive
> extrovert to be financially successful, but it helps. Espe-
> cially for men, ours is an outer-directed culture that
> rewards us for remaining strangers to ourselves, unac-
> quainted with feeling, intuition, or the subtleties of
> sensation and dreams.[8]

To find his identity, a man must cultivate a relationship
with the deeper part of himself, which involves not doing
more but doing less. It means creating special times and
places to be alone, to be quiet, to listen to the voices within,
to examine, grieve, and learn from one's emotional wounds,
to stand in the presence of God. Meditation, reading,
journaling, therapy, and a support group are a few ways to
nourish the soul. In the New Testament, Jesus knew the
value of time alone; he frequently withdrew from the
crowds to pray. By going down into his own inner darkness,
a man can become more aware of his feelings, his motivations, his needs, his desires, his hurts, and he can live more
actively, with a fuller sense of who he is. This process goes
on throughout life, and though it is not easy, it leads to
spiritual growth.

Third, *the movement challenges men to find strength and
support in the company of other men.* Our culture has taught us
that it's okay for men to play football or lift weights
together, but for some reason it's taboo for men to share
feelings with each other, especially their fears, hurts, and
longings. As a result, men end up burying their feelings or
else sharing them only with women. But women can only
understand up to a point; it takes other men to fully
empathize with a man's feelings. This is not an attempt to

exclude women or in any way minimize their contribution; it simply means that a man can only learn the stuff of masculinity from other men, especially from older men who have undergone the spiritual discipline of initiation themselves.

In the initiation rites of primitive cultures, it was always older men who ushered boys from the world of their mothers into the community of men. Through solemn, often elaborate ceremonies packed with symbolism and emotion, these older men would reveal to the boys all the spiritual teachings of the culture such as the way the world was created and the sacred history of the tribe. Together the ceremonies and spiritual instruction by the men depicted a ritual death of the boys to their childhood way of life, and a rebirth to the responsible life of an adult man.

Today's young men, in contrast, have no meaningful rituals to help them become mature adults. High-school and college graduations are a weak attempt to recognize the transition and celebrate it, but they usually have no spiritual content. Church programs for young people that lead to a ceremony of "confirmation" (or some similar name) contain a great deal of spiritual content, but they rarely amount to more than memorizing a package of church doctrines. The information is valuable, but often seems like a rigid, closed system, strangely detached from everyday life and relationships and even from the person of God himself. Neither approach gives a young man (or woman) the emotional and spiritual guidance to move out of the safe world of childhood and into the treacherous terrain of adulthood.

Nor do today's young men have older men nearby who care about their souls, who can infuse them with spiritual values. So in addition to getting support from others their own age, men are exhorted to seek out older, wiser men to serve as role models, counselors, mentors. An effective mentor can teach, challenge, guide, and bless a man in a different way than a man's father (though both are necessary). His care and spiritual concern call forth a clearer sense of one's self and a deeper, more mature masculinity.

In the Bible, Eli served as a mentor to young Samuel, as did Elijah to Elisha, Jesus to the disciples, and the apostle Paul to Timothy. We all need to seek out this kind of nurturing relationship with an older man. Though an actual relationship with a living man is preferable, it may be possible to be mentored by someone through their writing or teaching as well.

Fourth, *the men's movement uses myths, fairy tales, symbols, archetypes, rituals, dreams, art, and poetry to convey timeless truths and to bring about healing.* Since this aspect of the movement proves to be confusing for some and threatening for others, especially Christians, I'll devote more space to explaining it later in the book.

Finally, *the movement challenges men to reawaken the parts of themselves that have to do with initiative, forthrightness, clarity, resolve, respect for the earth, and connection to God.*

ANSWERING THE CRITICS

Before leaving this overview, I want to examine briefly some of the general public's responses to the movement. Much of the media coverage has focused on aspects of the movement that have immediate visual and emotional impact—men sitting in a circle drumming, "wildman" weekends where men run through the woods in a breechcloth carrying spears, men dancing and whooping with each other, men performing Native American rituals around a bonfire. Many men and women, after seeing these activities (or parodies of them) on TV or reading about them in magazines, believe that these startling images represent the core of what the men's movement is all about. Thankfully, it is not; only a small percentage of men are involved in these areas—a tiny branch on a huge tree. Yet this narrow media view, designed to sell more magazines and increase viewership, has led many men to ignore the movement and has outraged many women who think the movement is encouraging men to be more savage, violent, and macho. It has also caused many Christians to immediately brand the movement as new age or occultish.

I would be the last one to say that the men's movement is some kind of monolithic group in which all the participants believe and act the same way. Few if any movements in history have experienced absolute unanimity, including Christianity. No doubt some of the men who participate in these events really do believe that a facepaint job and a few weekends of romping in the woods will in itself revive their masculinity. On the other hand, some men may be trying to recover their identity by surrounding themselves with a stack of men's books, hoping they can study themselves into mature manhood. Both are mistaken.

There are many different men's groups, with many different activities and emphases, as I described earlier in this chapter. A few drum or camp. Some study books. Some sponsor lectures and seminars. Some are therapy groups led by a paid professional. Most are simple sharing and support groups. But they are all whittling away at different aspects of one primary goal: to help men get in touch with their emotional/spiritual center. The process involves not just the mind but also the body, not just the head but also the heart. Not all approaches and emphases fit for everyone, but that is no reason to reject the movement's core truths.

I see a parallel in the Christian Church. A number of years ago I visited a church service in which some participants were shouting in tongues, waving arms, dancing in the aisles, and falling to the floor in an ecstatic trance. Though there were moments when I appreciated the freedom these worshipers felt, the format was definitely not my style. But after the service, I didn't find myself saying, "Wow—

Christianity must not be true after all." I simply realized that people of different cultures and backgrounds, even Christian people, seek out many different kinds of environments to express their relationship to God. Church denominations have a variety of styles, formats, emphases, even doctrines, while still remaining faithful to the core truth about Christ. But they don't all fit for everyone, and that's fine.

The men's movement is similar. If we recognize its central purposes as I've outlined above, and if we use discernment, we can plug into the aspects of the movement that fit for us, that stir our souls most. As Christian men, we can tap the resources that help us move toward maturity without forcing us to compromise our faith. We can also organize groups in our churches that explore men's issues in a Christian context, as I am attempting to do in this book. If we are truly, humbly seeking to grow, both as Christians and as men, we can believe that God will be working in us to bring about that growth.

Not only has the movement raised the eyebrows of many men; it has also aroused the ire of many women, who feel that it is a throwback to the old patriarchal system of male dominance and power. They also disapprove of gatherings and conferences designed exclusively for men. Their response is understandable, given the many centuries of women suffering at the hands of men. As powerful a force as feminism has been, the inequities between men and women are only beginning to be corrected. Now that some men are trying to gain a clearer picture of who they are in the midst of today's social upheaval, it's easy to see why some women may view the movement as a "backlash" against feminism. Unfortunately, most of these concerns appear to stem from sensational media coverage or a knee-jerk reaction by some feminists rather than from a close look at the movement's true goals.

At this writing, Susan Faludi's book *Backlash* has been the most visible example of some women's scorn for the men's movement. The author takes numerous swipes, professional and personal, at Robert Bly and the men's movement in general.

In *The New York Times Book Review*, Jill Johnston writes that Bly's agenda for men "depends strictly on women playing their traditional roles at home," and that "male initiation always has to do with gender distinctions and the devaluation of women."[9] Yet Bly says the following in the preface to *Iron John*: "I want to make clear that this book does not seek to turn men against women, nor to return men to the domineering mode that has led to repression of women and their values for centuries. The thought in this book does not constitute a challenge to the women's movement."[10]

Many of the harder-line feminists base their criticism on the belief that men and women have no real differences, only culturally conditioned ones. Therefore, they say, it is destructive for men to search for their masculine identity because there really is no such thing as a masculine identity. There is only humanity.

Tammy Bruce of the National Organization for Women condemns the men's movement as follows: "The idea that you are not a man, that you are not masculine, unless you work to embody masculinity is frightening and ultimately dangerous. Men's attempts to be real men lead to confusion, frustration, and misery.... A degrading movement geared to spiral men even further down into an extreme that advocates primal behavior and a separatist philosophy is flourishing. This so-called men's movement advocates ideas that drive men further away from equity and understanding"[11] No doubt there are some men somewhere who fit this description, but these men bear no resemblance to the many thousands who are exploring men's issues with honesty, integrity, and respect for women. Again, Bruce's criticism implies that there are no differences between men and women, and that it is entirely inappropriate for men to explore what makes them uniquely masculine. I strongly disagree with this view.

I would answer these criticisms simply by stating my current understanding of male-female differences. Rather than view women and men as identical, I prefer to think of them as different but equal, and that we can both celebrate and attempt to bridge our differences. I would echo the opinion of Deborah Tannen, author of *You Just Don't Understand: Women and Men in Conversation,* who writes in the book's preface:

> To desire to affirm that women are equal has made some scholars reluctant to show they are different, because differences can be used to justify unequal treatment and opportunity. Much as I understand and am in sympathy with those who wish there were no differences between women and men—only reparable social injustice—my research, others' research, and my own and others' experience tell me it simply isn't so.[12]

Regarding the accusations of separatism and exclusivism, they go hand in hand with the extreme feminist belief in the sameness of men and women. If indeed they are the same, then there would be no need for men or women to do anything separately. But if they are equal but different, then there can be great value in men getting together occasionally with other men (and women with women) to discover their deeper identity, the part of them that is not merely a role. As it is, men and women are together most of the time at work, home, or church. And even when men are together at the office or the ballgame, their interaction with each other is often superficial. The purpose of men-only gatherings is to break through the superficiality, to get past rigid roles, to do the inner emotional/spiritual work that only they can do, to restore balance between their inner and outer selves. This kind of activity between men is not a revival of the "old-boy network"; instead, it helps these men to be more alive, conscious, and authentic persons in their everyday relationships with women and with other men.

In this chapter I've tried to show how the men's movement came to be and something of what it's like and what it emphasizes. I hope I've made it clear that the movement is not a backlash against women or a return to the hollow, macho-male stereotypes, but rather an attempt by men to take responsibility for their lives, both inner and outer. Now it's time to look at some of the ways this movement has helped me and other men in our journey from passivity to a more vital, conscious, active life.

Four

Breaking the Trance

And I know I'm miserable, can't you see
I just want you to be just like me
Boys grow up to be grown men
And then men change back into boys again....

When I was your age, I thought I hated my dad
And the feeling was a mutual one that we had.
We fought each other day and night.
I was always wrong, he was always right,
But he had the power and he needed to win—
His life half over, mine about to begin;
I'm not sure about that Oedipal stuff,
But when we were together it was always rough....

It never really ends though each race is run,
This thing between a father and a son;
Maybe it's power, push and shove;
Maybe it's hate, probably it's love.
Maybe it's hate, probably it's love.

                    —Loudon Wainwright III

Within five minutes of the time I first landed upon the Robert Bly/Bill Moyers TV special, I knew that my life could not stay the same. Something in me that had been stuck for a long time was opening—a trap door between my passive nice-guy exterior and my deeper, more turbulent but truer inner self. The male issues Bly spoke about—alienation from one's father, overconnection to one's mother, the need to move from boyhood to manhood—stirred many feelings in me from underneath that trap door. If I was to break out of my passivity and move into a more active kind of living, I realized I would have to crawl through that door and explore what was down there.

Well, I've been exploring for the past two years, and I feel amazed at how many discoveries I've made and how much of myself there is yet to know. But I've come to understand and accept myself a lot more, and I've even made some progress in overcoming passivity. In this chapter and the next two, I'll describe some of my own attempts to access the deeper, hidden parts of myself and how these encounters have helped me gain a greater sense of identity, purpose, and passion.

FINDING THE FATHER

At the beginning of this book, I mentioned the rattle that occurs in men during their thirties and forties. Usually it's a sign that a man's old habits and perceptions aren't working any more. One major emphasis of the men's movement is to reevaluate the patterns and beliefs we

105

picked up from our parents so that we can consciously make our own choices, that is, become mature men. When I finally began to listen to the rattle in my own gut, the first message I heard was, "It's time to look at your relationship with your father." To which I responded, "What relationship?"

For most of my life, it seemed, my father and I had knocked heads on everything. He seemed tense and irritated much of the time. He frequently lost patience with me as a child when I tried to help him with projects and didn't do it "right." During my teenage years in the late 1960s and early 1970s, we always seemed to get into arguments about issues—political issues such as the Vietnam War and ERA, and "moral" issues such as how long I could grow my hair and whether I could go to church without wearing a tie. These debates ended the same way every time: He talked the loudest, was always right (everyone else, including me, was wrong), and always had the last word; I felt very stupid, gave up in frustration, and retreated to my room in tears. Though I always believed Dad loved me, I got angry at him for not showing it more clearly. Once I lashed out at him and said, "You don't really love us kids—you just buy things for us!" I got to the point where I basically wrote him off, believing he had nothing to offer me. And yet I so badly wanted his acceptance and approval.

By the time I graduated from college and got married, I had learned to be civil with Dad. I generally avoided sensitive subjects, and when we did get into debates, I tended to bow out early. There were times along the way that I felt his support, such as when I went through my divorce, but our relationship did not really change in any significant way. An outsider might have thought we actually had a decent adult relationship. In reality, I hadn't even tried to understand this mysterious man who had helped to give me life. Nor had I seriously examined the effects (both positive and negative) he had on me. Instead, I had chosen to remain angry at him. My brothers and I would complain about him to each other and to my mother. I concluded that my relationship with him would improve only if *he* changed.

During this time, whenever someone asked me about my family, I'd say, "Well, I'm really close with my mother, but not at all close with my father." Indeed, the last person in the world I wanted to be like was my father. But in my occasional reflective moments, I couldn't deny that I was falling into many of the same habits and patterns that I disliked in him, including passivity and moodiness. I felt more and more afraid of the person I was becoming, yet powerless to do anything about it. It didn't occur to me that my own freedom and independence would first require me to move toward my father rather than away from him. Because we had never really bonded with each other, I was finding it impossible to separate from him emotionally so I could live my own life.

Early in 1989, my dad's father died of cancer. I had remarried by this time, and Nancy and I drove to northern Virginia for the funeral. Dad and I had several opportunities to talk about his final days with Grandpa. I knew Dad's upbringing had not been easy, but I wasn't aware of how many unresolved issues and feelings had remained between him and his father. Thankfully, they spent many hours together in the hospital going over past hurts, misunderstandings, and regrets, asking forgiveness of each other, reaffirming their love, and saying other things that needed to be said.

As I listened to Dad tell of these last encounters with Grandpa, I felt grateful that he was able to have that experience. But I also felt a strong conviction rising in me: I did not want to wait until Dad was on his deathbed to work out my difficulties with him. I wanted to know him, understand him, and accept him now, while there was still plenty of adult life left.

Taking this step of moving toward my father would help me greatly, I figured, but another part of me sensed that Dad would benefit too. I expressed my desire to him, and with a mixture of surprise, relief, and apprehension, he said he would like that very much. Since then, we've talked many times on the phone and in person, mostly about day-to-day goings on in our lives, but also about past memories and feelings. I feel so much more relaxed when we talk than I used to, because I'm no longer trying to win an argument or prove that I'm better or smarter than he is. We still don't agree on everything, but I allow him to have his own opinions, without trying to tell him he's wrong. Being right is no longer as important to me as being real.

Letting go of my anger and initiating an adult relationship with Dad created a wonderful by-product: I also found myself letting go of some mistaken impressions I'd had of him. I began to view him in a more balanced way, as a human being who not only wounded me in some ways, but who also was there for me in many ways that I hadn't previously acknowledged. Unlike many fathers I'd heard about, Dad attended my Little League baseball games, ninth-grade football games, school plays, and choir concerts. He took the family on numerous camping trips and long hikes in the Blue Ridge mountains. He and I built model airplanes, constructed a room-sized Lionel train layout, and assembled a large coin collection together. When I was in fourth or fifth grade, he bought a ping-pong table and taught my brother Brad and me how to play. At first he slammed the ball at us mercilessly, but before long we got the knack and began to beat him. We had loads of fun. Eventually he built us a large recreation room behind the house to put the table in.

As I started eighth grade, he showed me how to use a

35mm camera and how to process my own photos. Together
we built a darkroom in each of three different houses we
lived in, and spent many hours developing film and making
prints. I remember many Friday and Saturday nights of
playing Rook with Dad, Mom, Brad, and a big bowl of
potato chips. I also established some kind of musical
connection with Dad, because he always had records playing
in the house, and I liked it. Though he didn't share my rock-
'n'-roll tastes (he usually prefers classical), he bought and
wore out virtually every Peter, Paul and Mary album and
several Simon and Garfunkels, which I thoroughly enjoyed.
So without working too hard, I realized that I had quite a
few fond memories and connections with my father.

As much as I've savored those memories, I've also been
able to ask him about difficult times between us. We
compared notes on what was going on for us at various
times in my past and in his past. For instance, I told him of
the hurt I felt as a child when he would say, "You're not
sorry—you're careless!" He apologized, explaining that it
was the only way he knew how to teach. He described how
his father had treated him similarly; the phrase Dad grew up
hearing was, "You'll never amount to anything!" and he
admitted that it had hurt him too. Talking about these
feelings with Dad helped me understand both myself and
him better; and while it didn't erase the fact that I'd been
hurt, it gave me a context for finding healing. I realized that
I wasn't the only guy in the world with a past: my father had
a past, and his father, and so on. He received character gifts
and character wounds as well. Dad did the best he could
with the upbringing he was given; there was never reason to
question his love for me, or my value to him.

Hearing more about Dad's upbringing, along with the
significant events and people that molded his life, has also
helped me gain perspective. I've begun to see the reasons
for many of his strengths and weaknesses, and how many of

them were passed on to me. For instance, I had always thought that Dad only cared about boring, practical, intellectual things, and that I wanted to be creative and "artsy" with my life. But as he told me about his own youthful interests and desires, I began to wonder if we were much more similar on the inside.

He grew up in the factory town of Kenosha, Wisconsin, where his father was an assembly-line foreman at the Simmons furniture plant. Unlike many of his friends and relatives who assumed they too were destined for the factories, Dad felt a hunger for something more. As a young teenager he would hang out at the Coast Guard station on Lake Michigan, gazing at the waters for hours, often staying for the overnight watch on weekends. He also became interested in photography, and at age fourteen he worked in a camera shop after school, learning all he could. When someone dropped off their film for processing, the shop owner handed it to my dad, who took it into a darkroom in back and developed each print by hand. Within several years Dad had acquired a great deal of skill with a camera and in the darkroom, and wanted to pursue photography as a career. Judging by old enlargements he showed me of exquisite landscapes and striking portraits, I could see why. And I also understood how Dad wordlessly passed on to me his hunger for a life of depth and his desire to be involved with beauty and creativity.

So why didn't he pursue a photographic career, I wondered. His answer revealed a deep wound he had received late in his teenage years. One day he spoke to the Navy recruiter about the possibility of doing photography for the military. The recruiter assured him that the Navy was the perfect place for a budding photographer, and that if he enlisted, he would be sent to a special Navy photo school for further training. Just what Dad was looking for! Not only would he be able to follow his interests, get away from home and see the world, but he'd get paid for it—and his training and experience would be a virtual ticket to a good photography job when he got out. Excitedly he signed on the dotted line and prepared for the career of his dreams.

During boot camp, Dad received some devastating news that would alter the course of his life. The Navy had decided to shut down its photography school. He would have to choose a different track. Dad was stunned. What could he do? He had already enlisted and couldn't quit. So instead of shooting military maneuvers and making his own enlargements, Dad shot X rays and made hospital beds in the medical corps. By the time he left the Navy he had given up on his dream. He took business courses and became an insurance salesman.

I believe the Navy's treatment of my father inflicted a wound to his soul. His government, in whom he had placed his trust, had in effect cheated him and robbed him of his future. Certainly this was neither the first nor the only wound Dad had received; as a child he had suffered others from his own parents. But the Navy cut deeply. From that point on, a strong guiding principle in his life seemed to be, "Forget about what you really want in life; you'll probably get the rug pulled out from underneath you anyway. Just submit to the Organization and do what you're told."

During my growing-up years I noticed this attitude arising whenever Dad's job duties changed and especially when he was transferred to another city. Like many men of his generation, he basically assumed he had no choice but to follow orders. When I looked for summer jobs in high school, he would say, "Verne, if the only job you can find is digging ditches, you should be thrilled at the opportunity to work and earn college money." I frequently saw him looking bothered, and though I couldn't verbalize it as a boy, I sensed Dad begrudgingly believed that life would always be a pain and there was nothing he could do about it but keep a step ahead of the other guy, and look for loopholes in the System whenever he could. And though my life has taken a different path than his, I have carried his anger around in me too.

By the time I grew up and commuted to office jobs every day for more than a decade, I began to understand much more clearly the anger and frustration a man can feel as part of today's workaday world. It's a world in which we can't always achieve the kind of life we really want. At times I felt tempted to bow to the pressure, to simply give up my identity and let the rest of the world run my life for me. At the end of a particularly difficult day at the office, I said to myself on numerous occasions—without saying it—that I was done with taking responsibility for today and that I'd be just fine if I didn't have to help with dinner or play with my son or do anything but lie around and read a magazine. And yet I also felt guilt and sadness and grief as I did this, because I genuinely wanted to participate in the life of my family.

I now realize that at some level, I was experiencing the same inner conflict my father must have felt. All those nights when he came home angry and kept to himself, he didn't do it because I was a difficult kid, or because he didn't like me or wanted to hurt me, but because he was doing all he could do to cope with a life that fell way short of his original hopes. As I learned more about Dad's desires and disappointments in life, I came to understand why he was passive in many ways, and why I have been passive. And I've found it much easier to forgive him for his shortcomings.

All of this "father work" I've described here is aimed at establishing a conscious bond between father and son, one that goes beyond childhood misconceptions to a deeper reality. I'm not talking about denying the wounds we've received or attempting to recast our fathers into saints. Rather I'm saying that we need to accept our fathers as they are and as they were, affirming the good they gave us and forgiving the bad. By coming to terms with his father, a man can begin to feel a connection to his own male identity. Instead of blindly, passively repeating his father's mistakes, he can begin to make active choices about the path his life and his character will take. That's what I'm trying to do now.

This process will be different for every man, since no two father-son relationships are the same. Several men in my support group have never even seen their fathers, who died or abandoned them before they were born. Others have grown up with violent or rageful fathers, stepfathers, uncles, grandfathers, or no father-figure at all. Establishing a father bond in these circumstances is much more difficult, but I believe it is possible. Most fathers (or father-figures) gave their sons something of value, even if they were absent themselves. A roof over their head, a decent standard of living, food on the table, money for college, whatever. At the very least, every man's father gave him the gift of life; isn't this precious gift worth being thankful for? For those who can remember nothing but extreme abuse or neglect by their fathers, the work may involve recognizing that their fathers probably didn't want to be that way, that they were most likely abused or neglected themselves and never learned healthy ways of living or parenting. In any case, the goal is to forgive and let go.

One further way that finding my father has helped me: I am looking more closely at the kind of father I am to my own thirteen-year-old son, Brendan. In my relation to him, I neither want to be passive, automatically doing the same things my father did to me, nor reactive, doing the opposite of whatever my father did; what I'm trying to strive for is making active, conscious choices about what I think is best for my son. This gets difficult because Brendan lives 2,000 miles away, and though we talk on the phone twice a week, we only see each other for several weeks out of the year. So in spite of the distance, I'm working at being a more responsible father.

DECLARING INDEPENDENCE FROM MOTHER

In my family, there is no question that all three of us boys were closer to Mom than to Dad. We always spent more time with her, talked about all our problems with her, and shared more affection with her. She was indeed a Supermom to all of us. I'm sure that her love and attention have benefited me in many ways: She has helped me to be a good listener, to empathize with people, to have a good nurturing instinct. Until recently, I never questioned for a minute that my relationship to her was anything but the perfect model for all parent-child relationships. In my mind, Dad was the problem because he wasn't like Mom.

Then came the rattle. Its first message to me was about Dad, but soon thereafter it spoke up again: "Uh, Verne— better look at your relationship with your mother too." I needed to ask similar questions about her that I had asked about Dad: Were all my perceptions of her accurate? Did I blindly accept everything she told me? Have I unwittingly picked up some unhealthy habits or patterns from her? Were there aspects of our relationship that wounded me in some way?

At this point I am still in the midst of exploring these questions. But so far I can speak of two discoveries. First, I have come to realize that the closeness my brothers and I shared with my mother amounted to an unconscious alliance against my father. No one ever sat down and said, "Okay, let's get him!"—it just happened. Mom saw that Dad wasn't as available to us (physically or emotionally) as he could be, and she tried to step into the gap. What mother would have done anything different? Unfortunately, the inadvertent alliance had a damaging side-effect on me: I was further closed off from the chance to develop my own relationship to Dad, to form my own opinions about him—and about my own masculinity. By processing everything through my mother, including everything about my father, I only had her view of him to go on—a view that was legitimate for her, but very one-sided for me. Dad had made it difficult enough for me to know him, but Mom, without realizing it, had made it even more so.

Second, I discovered that I still have unfinished business with Mom in an important area: emotional separation. Unlike my relationship with Dad, I had easily bonded with my mother. But I had never really separated from her—or from my "mother complex"—to become an independent person and, in particular, an emotionally balanced man. I've allowed my psyche to be dominated by the influences of my mother, as well as those of some abstract feminine power. This excessive influence has carried over into my relationships, leading me to project many unrealistic and unfair expectations on women. In a way I want them to be like my mother, or like some Great Mother who will care for me and solve all my problems and make everything better. As a young child, it's good for me to look to my mother, but as an adult, I need to care for myself and take charge of my own problems. By staying too connected to my mother, I set myself up for a passive approach to life, expecting others—my first wife, women in general—to bring me meaning and fulfillment and a sense of identity. It didn't work.

Making a clean break, however, is far from easy. I and other men I've talked to still feel a strong bond of faithfulness to our mothers. I don't want to hurt her feelings or give the impression that I don't love her any more. She, on the other hand, doesn't want to "lose" me, because I've been there for her in many ways over the years too. But what I'm realizing, along with other men, is that separating emotionally from my mother is an essential step I must take

in order to reach mature manhood. In the Iron John fairy
tale, the boy discovers he must steal the key from under his
mother's pillow before he can leave the castle.

Robert A. Johnson puts it this way:

> No son ever develops into manhood without being
> disloyal to his mother in some way. If he remains with his
> mother to comfort her and console her then he never gets
> out of his mother complex. Often a mother will do all she
> can to keep her son with her. One of the most subtle ways
> is to encourage in him the idea of being loyal to mother,
> but if he gives in to her completely on this score then she
> often winds up with a son who has a severely injured
> masculinity. The son must ride off and leave his mother,
> even if it seems to mean disloyalty, and the mother must
> bear this pain. Later, like Parsifal [the legendary seeker of
> the Holy Grail], the son may then come back to the
> mother and they may find a new relationship on a new
> level, but this can only be done after the son has first
> achieved his independence and transferred his affections
> to a woman of his own age.[1]

Right now I would say I'm somewhere in the middle of
accomplishing that separation. I find myself projecting
fewer motherly expectations on Nancy, and I am trying to
relate to her and to myself in a more balanced way. I also
deeply desire to "find a new relationship on a new level"
with my mother, and I believe that in time we will do so.

The universal need of a child to separate from both
parents (after bonding with them) has been confirmed by
psychologists around the globe. As I've come to realize that
need in myself, I've gained a new appreciation for the classic
biblical passage about marriage proclaimed at every wedding: "A man will leave his father and mother and be united
to his wife, and they will become one flesh" (Genesis 2:24).
The "leaving" means more than a physical leaving, more
than moving across town or even across the country. It
means leaving behind their authority over our life, at both
the conscious and unconscious levels. We must continue to

honor and respect our parents, but we must learn to separate ourselves from them emotionally in order to take responsibility for our own life.

Jesus' words in Luke 14:26–27 add a further dimension: "If anyone comes to me and does not hate his father and mother, his wife and children, his brothers and sisters—yes, even his own life—he cannot be my disciple. And anyone who does not carry his cross and follow me cannot be my disciple." Hate in this passage does not mean literal hatred, but rather "loving less," keeping in proper perspective. We cannot allow our connections with those close to us—parents, siblings, spouses, children—to get in the way of our relationship to our own self, and especially, to God. Jesus seems to be describing a chain of priorities: Our relationships with those close to us must be less important than our own life and selfhood; and ultimately, we must be willing to submit our own selves to the power of God.

THE VALUE OF THE WOUND

I have spoken throughout this book about the wounds a man receives from his parents, from society, from nature, and so on. These wounds often prevent him from completing the bonding and separating process with his parents. For a man to arrive at a balanced relationship with his parents, and move forward with his life, it is essential that his inner wounds be inspected. Some leaders in the men's movement have made an intriguing observation about these wounds that seems to fit here: When a man's wound is properly examined and integrated into his life, it will often turn out to be his greatest gift. In Robert Bly's words:

> Where a man's wound is, that is where his genius will be. Wherever the wound appears in our psyches, whether from alcoholic father, shaming mother, shaming father, abusing mother, whether it stems from isolation, disabil-

ity, or disease, that is precisely the place for which we will give our major gift to the community.[2]

Biblical accounts seem to confirm the value of a wound. Jacob received a wound after wrestling with the angel that was to serve as a permanent reminder of his encounter with God (Genesis 32:22–32). The apostle Paul spoke of a "thorn in my flesh," some kind of physical or emotional ailment which tormented him. When he repeatedly asked God to remove it, God told him no: "He said to me, 'My grace is sufficient for you, for my power is made perfect in weakness'" (2 Corinthians 12:9). Perhaps the supreme example of a wound's redeeming value is in Jesus Christ: "He was pierced for our transgressions, he was crushed for our iniquities; the punishment that brought us peace was upon him, and by his wounds we are healed" (Isaiah 53:5).

As I reflect on how my wounds have had a positive effect on me, one possibility comes to mind. In many ways, I received a wound in the area of communication. I never learned as a child to communicate my feelings or my needs clearly and directly. It just wasn't done in my family. All too often I relied on assumptions, indirect manipulation, sarcasm, and nonverbal means to get my point across. I depended on my mother and others to pick up on what I needed without my having to ask for it. Now, as an adult, I find myself drawn to a career in writing—a precise form of communication. Could it be that my wound was the seed of that desire?

MEN AND MENTORS

Becoming a mature man depends heavily on how completely we can bond and separate from our parents and how well we can learn from the wounds we received. The task is especially difficult, however, for men who grew up with absent and abusive fathers. Not only do we fail to learn what masculinity is like from our fathers, but we find ourselves alienated from other men who could teach us, especially older men. One man in the Monday night support group explained his predicament as follows:

> I am terrorized and afraid of men, and specifically one man, my father. He was a very nasty brutal man. He was in the military, and he needed to be in the military in order to survive because he had a very nasty childhood himself. But his legacy to me was terror, psychological warfare, shame, guilt, and other things. And that colors all my relationships with men today. When I look at a man, I somehow still see my father. And I don't like that any more. I know also there's a dichotomy within myself. I'm tall and pretty big, and I have this deep voice, so I give this projection of being rather powerful on the outside. But on the inside, all the warning bells, all the emotional bells go off whenever I deal with men. I think, "Where's the next abuse coming from, the next aggressive act against me, and how bad is it going to be?" And I don't want that any more either.

Though many of us may not fear being abused by other men, we tend to carry a certain attitude of caution or suspicion toward them. We share little if any of our inner selves with each other, preferring to interact at the surface level, talking about common interests, work, or sports. And we expect little in return. We also tend to dismiss the opinions of older men, writing them off as out-of-touch fuddy-duddies, yet forgetting that we ourselves are now middle-aged. With this kind of dynamic prevailing between ourselves and other men, how can we ever learn the inside story of what it means to be a man? How can we learn what makes a man tick? And most important, how can I discover the mature man in me, the man who knows who he is and what he must do with his life?

Throughout history, a man has always needed something in addition to his father to help him reach his full masculine potential. This is true even for men who had good fathers. What does a man need? The presence of other men, in particular older men, who care about his inner, spiritual self. Think about it: Our fathers had to make it their first priority to shelter, feed, and clothe us. Without these things, we wouldn't be around to get our intellectual, emotional, and spiritual needs met. These were secondary from the fathers' standpoint, and so they failed to see who we were on the inside or failed to see us completely. That is why, in order to activate a man's deeper self, a mentor must enter the picture.[3]

A mentor usually is an older man (though not necessarily old in years) who has something in common with the younger man—the same vocation or avocation, for instance. He could be a "sage" in one's area of work, a relative, a longtime friend of the family, a college professor, a youth-group leader, an elder or minister in the church, a sponsor from a Twelve-Step group.

Several things distinguish a mentor from other older men. First, a mentor has a certain wisdom that he has gained during his life that the younger man can learn from. In some way he stands out as a role model. Often this comes from working in the same field. Second, he's much more interested in what's going on inside rather than outside of the younger man; in other words, he cares about the man's soul and tries to nourish it. He helps a man to focus on what's really important. Third, the mentor is a "seer" in the sense that he sees things that the man may not be able to see in himself—blind spots and shortcomings, but also strengths and gifts. He is able to remain impartial about these traits, however, because he doesn't carry the emotional baggage of the man's father. He can simply call attention to them to help the man grow. Sometimes he advises, sometimes he challenges, sometimes he criticizes; but it is clear that he does it out of concern for the man's inner development. Fourth, and closely related to the third, a mentor gives the man a sense of being recognized and a hint of where his destiny may lie. He calls forth greatness from the man.

No one man may possess all these traits, but every mentor has some of them. In college I spent many hours with my writing professor, Paul Fromer, who also advised the college newspaper I worked on. Though I didn't do well in his class, I felt that he saw some kind of potential in me as a writer and editor. His advice, encouragement, and support grew as I became editor of the college paper. During the time we worked together, I learned not only about the craft of writing but also about excellence and integrity, and I came to believe that perhaps I could achieve those things in my life. I can't identify a particular time or place that it happened, but I do know that Paul recognized something in me, and for that I am grateful.

There is no formula for how a mentor can activate a man's soul and validate his gifts, but usually the young man knows, sooner or later, when it has happened. In 1904, a man who had been corresponding with the great poet Rainer Maria Rilke sent some of his poems to him. Rilke's wonderful response shows both the beauty of recognition and the importance of a man receiving it from a respected mentor:

> I have copied your sonnet, because I found that it is lovely and simple and born in the form in which it moves with such quiet decorum. It is the best of those of your poems that you have let me read. And now I give you this copy because I know that it is important and full of new experience to come upon a work of one's own again written in a strange hand. Read the lines as though they were someone else's, and you will feel deep within you how much they are your own.[4]

How does a man go about finding a mentor? A way to start is by thinking of men we admire, men who could serve as a role model. What men do we know who are wise, independent, not swayed by every wind of opinion, who live a creative, original life, who have faced their own demons, and who care about the world of the soul? It may not be easy to think of someone right away, but in time, one or more men may come to mind or may come into our life or may even be right under our nose. It's scary to begin a mentor relationship in today's society, because it so rarely occurs naturally as in centuries past (with tradesmen and apprentices, for example). But taking that first step of establishing contact can make a real difference. I believe there are many wise men around who long for the chance to cultivate a younger man's mind and soul, but don't know exactly where to look. Somehow the older and younger men need to seek out each other.[5]

In building a relationship with a mentor, it's important not to make him into a father-figure. One of the great advantages of an effective mentor is precisely that he is not the man's father. Fathers are too likely to step in and control their sons or too susceptible to taking their son's mistakes as a reflection on them. They can't be objective. A mentor, on the other hand, didn't change your diapers and didn't see you picking up on his bad habits. He can call the shots as he sees them. But if a man projects the image of his father onto the mentor and expects the mentor to meet the needs his father never met, problems will arise. While a mentor can help a younger man resolve some of his father issues, he cannot and should not try to step into the father's role.

I've been fortunate to have experienced several kinds of mentors in my life. Some have been professors, and some have been trusted friends in publishing. Some, such as M. Scott Peck and Robert Bly, I have experienced through their books, lectures, and tapes. I would even say that musician Van Morrison has served as a mentor, as I feel I've established a relationship with him through his music and lyrics. All of these people, even those I haven't met personally, have not only imparted wisdom to me, but have helped me to recognize things about myself that have enhanced my growth.

By far the most significant one has been my therapist, Earl Laman, whom I've known for seventeen years. We talk only once a week for an hour, and he doesn't know much about the everyday details of my life, but he "sees" me and knows me better than any man I have ever met. This did not happen instantly, of course; in fact, when I first began seeing him I thought of him more as a resource person, someone who could answer my questions and solve my problems. But once we had established an ongoing relationship, I realized that he wasn't going to fix my problems; instead, he wanted me to recognize that I had the potential to solve my own. He helped me to see that the resources for living an active, growing life were within me, not in someone else. His role has been that of the honest, caring facilitator. As a result, I have grown tremendously in many areas of my life. A deep love has grown between us over the years, and I will always cherish our relationship.

MEN SUPPORTING EACH OTHER

Not only can a mentor put us in touch with our true self, but other men our own age can also play a part. It is a different part, but nevertheless an extremely valuable one. When a man begins to share his deep feelings, hurts, fears, and joys with other men, individually or in a group, it has a profound effect on his soul. Perhaps for the first time in his life, he realizes that his feelings are okay and do not have to be suppressed. He is able to gain perspective on his own struggles as a man by listening to other men talk about theirs. And the perspective he attains is uniquely male, something he cannot get from a woman or even his wife. At numerous times of difficulty in my life, I've thought, "No one knows what it's like to go through what I'm going through." But in the men's group I attend, I've found that many others—whether ten years younger or twenty years older—indeed understand what I'm going through. Sometimes, possibly because of the Western doctrine of self-sufficiency, I don't believe anyone else has something to say that will help me with my problems, and I don't believe sharing my experiences will help anyone else. But then I sit down with fifteen other men for an hour or two, and I find that there is great wisdom in telling our stories to each other.

There's another valuable dimension to meeting with other men that I would call the "ritual dimension." I've spoken about how today's men have few if any rituals to help them move from boyhood to manhood. In primitive tribes, initiation rituals were a standard part of the culture, and they always involved groups of men. A boy could not simply say to himself, "Okay, I'm no longer a boy—it's time for me to be a man." The boy had to undergo certain rituals, and furthermore, he had to do them in the presence of other men. Again, there is the need for recognition of the boy's inward transformation by the male community. The boy is no longer a boy; he has died to boyhood and been reborn into manhood. When this group recognition occurs, the boy experiences the change in himself with much greater power and depth.

To some degree, this can happen in men's groups. Some have even designed their own rituals for men to complete the transition they never made into manhood. But even at the simplest level of sharing, the other men in a group can serve as "ritual witnesses" to the growth and change that is taking place in each other. I see it as quite similar to the practices of many churches, where those who want to join the community come forward to be confirmed. Baptism and the Eucharist have strong ritual and initiatory overtones. Recent converts often profess their faith publicly before the congregation, while others may give testimonies of God's work in their life. The practices all serve a similar two-fold purpose: to inspire and encourage the community, and to strengthen the effect of the change on the person himself.

The Monday Night Men's Support Group I attend has met for more than two years now. As I talk about my up-and-down journey from passivity to maturity, and as I listen to other men talk about theirs, I find myself feeling more determined to stay on the path, to keep moving forward. I count the friends I have made there as among the closest male friends I've ever had. Because they've been there for me, I've found it easier to forgive those in my past who haven't, beginning with my father. I truly believe that these men have helped me in a concrete way to draw closer to my true masculine identity.

Five

Snagging the Self

*It is easier to sail many thousands of miles
through cold and storm and cannibals, in
a government ship, with five hundred men
and boys to assist one, than it is to explore
the private sea, the Atlantic and Pacific
of one's own being alone.*

—Henry David Thoreau

Coming to terms with one's father and mother, taking time to be with other men, and building a relationship with a mentor are extremely important parts of a man's journey out of passivity. But the ongoing work to be done needs to occur in a man's relationship with himself—not only the external self he presents to the world, but the deeper inner self. Psychologists have known for some time that our conscious thoughts, feelings, and actions represent only a fraction of our total self—perhaps as little as 4 or 5 percent.[1] The rest lies under the trapdoor in our unconscious, the larger part of us that we don't know, or more accurately, the part that knows us better than we do.

Before looking under the trapdoor, however, it may be worthwhile to pause and ask a question: Why bother with all this talk about one's *self?* Isn't it egotistical, narcissistic, and contrary to what Christians and other decent people should be all about? There are a lot of hurting people and a lot of needs out there in the world. Shouldn't we concentrate on helping others instead of fretting over ourselves?

It's a good question. After all, Jesus does say, "If anyone would come after me, he must deny himself and take up his cross daily and follow me. For whoever wants to save his life will lose it, but whoever loses his life for me will save it" (Luke 9:23–24). Sounds pretty grim for the self-explorer— unless he goes on to read Jesus' very next sentence: "What good is it for a man to gain the whole world, and yet lose or forfeit his very self?" (9:25). Christ cannot be contradicting himself, so there must be a deeper meaning in this statement. I believe he is expressing two sides of the same truth that must be kept in balance with each other. On one hand, our self is small and insignificant compared to God and his purposes. But on the other hand, our self is more valuable than the whole world.[2]

Another relevant two-sided truth is the biblical command to "love your neighbor as yourself" (Leviticus 19:18). If our self is worthless and a waste of time to bother with, then it appears that we also have little responsibility to love our neighbor. Christian essayist and novelist Frederick Buechner writes:

> Love your neighbor as yourself is part of the great commandment. The other way to say it is, Love yourself as your neighbor. Love yourself not in some egocentric, self-serving sense but love yourself the way you would love your friend in the sense of taking care of yourself, nourishing yourself, trying to understand, comfort, strengthen yourself.[3]

Two sides of the same truth, but unless both sides are observed, the truth goes down the drain. The apostle Paul writes, "Each of you should look not only to your own interests, but also to the interests of others" (Philippians 2:4). Here it is again, the balancing act. Unfortunately, passive men have gone so far to one side, focusing so much on the interests, needs, and feelings of others, that they have lost their own selves in the process, or perhaps never even found their selves to start with. And how can you truly give your self to others and to God if you don't have one? In his book *Fire in the Belly,* Sam Keen writes:

> We cannot forget our self until we have remembered it. We remain a problem to ourselves—self-absorbed, compulsively introspective, and narcissistic—so long as we have no authentic self-love. It is only when we arrive at a deep sense of self-acceptance that we are able to be self-forgetting and spontaneous.[4]

So what I'm talking about in this book is not forsaking those around us, but rather restoring balance. The better we know ourselves, understand ourselves, and take care of ourselves, the better we will be able to give ourselves to others. We will bring a richer, truer, and healthier self to our wives, children, family, and friends.

GOING DOWN

Now it's time to open the trapdoor and look for the other 95 percent of ourselves. Actually, we can't even come close to knowing ourselves completely, but we can know a lot more than we know now. Carl Jung used the term "unconscious" to refer to the vast repository of information, images, memories, associations, values, emotions, and much more that lie under that door.

The unconscious contains many aspects of our selves, including (but not limited to) our dreams, fantasies, underlying motives, repressed feelings or events, family secrets, our "dark" side, our gut feelings, our imagination, our deepest desires, our greatest fears, and our strongest needs. It holds material common to all human beings, such as the part of us that resonates with universal symbols or archetypes, our connection to the earth and the animal kingdom, the stuff of masculinity and femininity. I also believe that the unconscious houses our spiritual side, or our soul, including the stamp of God's image (Genesis 1:27), our capacity for sin or wrongdoing (Romans 5:12), our knowledge of God's existence (as the Bible states in Romans 1:19–20), our conscience or sense of right and wrong (Romans 2:14–15), and the place in us where God may dwell (Luke 17:20–21).

When I say that passive men are "out of touch" with their feelings, their desires, their sense of identity, and God, I mean that we've allowed these things to stay buried in our unconscious. Sometimes we're unaware of them because of denial or repression; we all take various parts of ourselves that we're afraid of, that we don't like, or that others don't like, and banish them to our unconscious. Maybe we were never taught or shown that this deeper, truer part of ourselves deserves to be honored. The unconscious has tremendous wealth and wisdom and energy that it can give us—and in fact, wants to give us—if we will only take the time to listen. That's what the rattle I heard was all about: My unconscious was trying to alert me to something. It was trying to say that it (actually me, the deeper part of me) did not like the passive approach to life I was taking, and wanted me to do something about it. At that moment, and whenever the unconscious stirs, I am faced with a choice: to listen or not to listen.

There are many ways that we can listen to our unconscious. In the Iron John story, the boy is instructed to sit quietly next to a spring of water. For many centuries, the image of water or bodies of water has symbolized the depth and nourishment of the human soul. In the New Testament, Jesus had a conversation with a woman next to a well, and he did not hesitate to make the parallel between the water in the well and the "living water" of the soul that he could give (John 4:10–15). So if we want to find out what's in our soul and bring it up into our conscious life, we need to go fishing. I don't think it's any accident that at least seven of Jesus' disciples were fishermen. Though we're quick to describe their new role as fishing for other followers (Matthew 4:19), it's clear throughout the Gospels that the disciples also did a great deal of "soul-fishing," that is, searching their own inner lives. If we take the time to cast our lines into our own uncharted waters, we may just snag something of our true identity.

One way to do this is by keeping track of our dreams. By writing them down regularly, reflecting on their imagery, learning their symbolic language, noticing patterns in the story lines and parallels with our "waking" life, it's possible to learn a great deal about who we are, the direction our life is taking, or the direction it needs to take. Dreams (and visions, their close relative) occurred throughout the Bible, and they were consistently viewed as messages from God. "For God does speak—now one way, now another— though man may not perceive it," says Elihu in the book of Job. "In a dream, in a vision of the night, when deep sleep falls on men as they slumber in their beds" (Job 33:14–15). David in the Psalms writes, "I will praise the Lord, who counsels me; even at night my heart instructs me" (16:7). The early church also believed in the divine origin of dreams.[5]

Over the past ten years, I've had several significant dreams that stuck fast to my memory. As I explored their meaning with my therapist, I came to believe that they were indeed the voice of God speaking (symbolically) from within my soul, helping me to see myself more clearly. This past year I have tried to record my dreams on paper more regularly, and again I have been amazed at the wisdom and insight they've given me.

For example, in a number of dreams, all my movements had a robotic quality, as if I were some kind of automaton. At the time I had these dreams, I was struggling with a lack of initiative in my life. (I still wrestle with this, by the way.) To help me better understand what was happening, these dreams offered up a striking image of myself, merely going through the motions but not really making my own choices. When I stopped to think about my conscious life, I realized that I was doing exactly that—doing what others expected of me rather than listening to my own heart. The dreams had painted a picture of my own passivity.

Recently another dream came to me that could be called a "confirmation dream" or a "status report dream." Here it is, in part:

I am sitting on the couch in my living room, and lying next to me is a huge, live, ocean fish, probably three feet long. My apartment is on the second floor. I notice that the fish is growing larger as the day passes. I am completely comfortable with the fish's presence. I take it with me for a drive in the car and pull up to a rustic old building, possibly a restaurant. Then I carry the big fish down into a dank cellar, where there are more fish similar to mine lying to one side. In this cellar there are two large storage closets with old wooden doors; I intend to take my big fish into one of the closets and simply sit down with it, alone. When I look into the left-hand closet, I see piles of live stingrays and decide not to go in. In the right-hand closet, I see live octopuses and refuse to go in there either. Then I wake up.

What could a bizarre dream like this possibly mean? For the sake of simplicity, I'll skip over some of the details and go for the overview. First, the movement in the dream was downward, from the second floor apartment to the ground to the cellar below the ground. Second, the fish were all sea-dwelling fish. A brief summary of the dream's overall meaning could be that I am in the midst of a downward movement in my life. I am going down into my soul or unconscious, and I am discovering various aspects of my self that I didn't know before. Some of these discoveries frighten me and I don't appear ready yet to face them. But I do feel "at home" with at least one part of me, represented by the fish, and that part of me appears to be growing. (An additional thought: The fish is also an ancient symbol for Christ. Is it possible that I am drawing closer to Christ in some way or that my awareness of Christ's presence in my life is growing?)

Recording and reflecting on one's dreams is a remarkable (and sometimes disturbing) experience, but I highly recommend it as a profound means of self-discovery. The insight of a competent therapist can be of great help here, as well as books on dream analysis. John A. Sanford's *Dreams: God's Forgotten Language* is an excellent book to start with.

Another way a man can honor and listen to his unconscious is through what Robert Bly calls "kitchen work" or "ashes work," terms he derived from fairy tale imagery. In the Iron John story, the boy, whom we know to be a king's son, leaves the security of his parents and rides off on Iron John's shoulders. Everything seems great at first, but the boy eventually realizes he doesn't have any skills to support himself. He ends up working for a cook in the basement of another castle, carrying wood and water, and raking up ashes. This stage in a man's life has two primary characteristics: a descent or fall from status, and the experience of humility. Being fired or laid off from a job, getting divorced, taking a year off from college, landing in the hospital, getting trapped in an addiction—anything that causes a man to take a hard look at himself, reevaluate his life, get in touch with what's really important to him—these are all means of descent. And it is usually in the midst of some kind of descent that a man hears the "rattle." The downward turn stands in contrast to everything our culture and many of our churches tell us: that our task in life is to "rise above it all," "stay on top of things," "look at the bright side," "praise the Lord anyhow," and so on. Going down is the only way to bring our inner and outer selves into harmony with each other and with God.

Ashes work means being willing to face the parts of ourselves that have died, that is, turned to ashes: our boyish bravado that believed we could change the world, our hopes and dreams for great achievements and financial success. By admitting that we're not the big shots we thought we were, that our old ways of living and relating no longer work, that a fat paycheck did nothing to bring fulfillment, that our addictions and compulsions have gotten the best of us, we begin to experience genuine humility and grief. And in so doing, we recognize our need to submit to a power greater than ourselves, the power of God. In his profound book *Addiction and Grace,* Gerald G. May writes:

> Addiction teaches us not to be too proud. Sooner or later, addiction will prove to us that we are not gods. Then we will realize that we are our own worst enemies; we cannot beat ourselves. At that point, when we have exhausted all the available false repositories for our hope, it is possible that we will turn to God with a true sense of who we are, with an integrity that is both humble and confident, with a dignity that knows itself because it has met its limits.[6]

May's words apply not only to addictions, but to whatever it is in our life that has "turned to ashes." The key is to allow ourselves to remain in our lowly state long enough to listen to all of the feelings it will stir up in us. These are the feelings God can use to speak his saving word to us, and enable us to put our lives back on track. Take three common feelings of many men at the kitchen-and-ashes stage—stress, depression, and burnout. Sam Keen suggests in *Fire in the Belly* that rather than trying to avoid or "manage" these feelings, men should listen to them more closely:

> Stress is not simply a disease; it is a symptom that you are living somebody else's life, marching to a drumbeat that doesn't syncopate with your personal body rhythms, playing a role you didn't create, living a script written by an alien authority. Depression is more than low self-esteem; it is a distant early warning that you are on the wrong path and that something in you is being pressed down, beat on, kept imprisoned, dishonored. Burnout is nature's way of telling you you've been going through the motions but your soul has departed; you're a zombie, a member of the walking dead, a sleepwalker.[7]

So many of the feelings men experience at the kitchen-and-ashes stage relate to their work or career that it seems appropriate to look more closely at a deep need that lies within every man: to find his own unique vocation or calling in life.

THE CALL FROM WITHIN

As a fledgling editor just out of college, I remember meeting Philip Yancey at a conference. At the time he was editor of *Campus Life,* an award-winning youth magazine. When I asked where he and his staff got their ideas for articles, he said that they basically pursued whatever their individual interests were. By staying in touch with the questions and struggles of their own lives, he said, it was easy to connect with the world of young people through common feelings and needs. Philip was encouraging his staff, and me, to trust our instincts.

I have carried his advice with me ever since, but only recently did I realize that it applies not only to writing and editing, but to all of life. In today's world, and especially in today's church, men are generally discouraged from trusting their instincts or gut feelings. Instead, we are expected to do the "right" thing, choose the safest, most logical options, and follow the socially acceptable course in life, which is getting a degree, a job, a car, a wife, a promotion, a house, and a child—in that order. Veer from this course in any significant way, and our parents, company, or church think something's wrong with us.

Trusting our instincts is actually quite similar to the late mythologist Joseph Campbell's famous words (often quoted out of context): "Follow your bliss." What he did not mean by this statement is, "If it feels good, do it." Rather, he meant that we are to listen to and follow our deepest needs and desires for the kind of life we want to live, the vocation or calling we want to pursue, and so on. In 1903 German poet Rainer Maria Rilke answered a letter from a man who said he wanted to be a poet but didn't know if he was good enough. Rilke's words:

> You are looking outward, and that above all you should not do now. Nobody can counsel and help you, nobody. There is only one single way. Go into yourself. Search for the reason that bids you write; find out whether it is spreading out its roots in the deepest places of your heart, acknowledge to yourself whether you would have to die if it were denied you to write. This above all—ask yourself in the stillest hour of your night: *must* I write? Delve into yourself for a deep answer. And if this should be affirmative, if you may meet this earnest question with a strong and simple *"I must,"* then build your life according to this necessity; your life even into its most indifferent and slightest hour must be a sign of this urge and a testimony to it.[8]

Most passive men haven't yet gone through this kind of self-searching, which is needed not only for a life of writing or art, but for every life, because every man's life is a story he is writing, or a piece of art he is creating, whether he is an office administrator, construction worker, computer programmer, or farmer, or even if he is unemployed. It takes time and courage to look inward in this way. Perhaps it's too scary to do so, because a man might discover how far he has run from his own desires. He may feel like his life has been a failure or that he has wasted his college and graduate school education. Maybe it will only make him feel more depressed than he already is in his current work. Maybe he figures he's stuck in his present job and couldn't change even if he wanted to, so why bother going after a dream.

These are all genuine reasons to avoid turning inward. But they need to be confronted if a man wants to cut through the expectations of those around him and discover the one thing, the one calling, that gives him more passion for living than anything else. It may very well be the line of work he is pursuing right now, though not necessarily the precise job. But it's also possible that he will encounter a deep underlying desire for something completely different. This desire is holy, sent by God himself, and pleads for a man's tending. So regardless of the direction he feels called, he must hear that call from within. The self-awareness that results is of far more importance in the long run than any practical decision about a particular job or career track. Again, Rilke:

> Perhaps it will turn out that you are called to be an artist. Then take that destiny upon yourself and bear it, its burden and its greatness, without ever asking what recompense might come from outside. . . . But perhaps after this descent into yourself and into your inner solitude you will have to give up becoming a poet; (it is enough, as I have said, to feel that one could live without writing: then one must not attempt it at all). But even then this inward searching which I ask of you will not have been in vain. Your life will in any case find its own ways thence, and that they may be good, rich and wide I wish you more than I can say.[9]

The kind of soul-exploration I've been talking about here is not a one-time occurrence or something a man can complete in a weekend conference. It's a process that continues throughout his life, though some times may be more intense than others. And it's an active process that the man must initiate and take responsibility for. But it's absolutely necessary if a man wants to reclaim his sense of identity in work and in life. Exploring these issues and feelings with other men, and especially with a mentor, can be extremely valuable.

THE SHADOW

After my father taught me how to shoot and process my own photos in eighth grade, I carried a camera with me nearly everywhere I went, through most of high school and two years of college. I shot for the school paper, the school yearbook, the local weekly newspaper, and just for fun. I found myself fascinated with shadows and often photographed interesting shadow patterns. I noticed that portraits had a fuller, more three-dimensional character when they included shadows. Many times I would stand with my back to the sun and allow my own shadow to intrude into the photo. And when I was photo editor of one of my college yearbooks, the picture I chose of myself for the staff page was a self-portrait of my shadow.

I can't explain exactly what intrigued me so much about shadows, but something in me knew that my shadow represented a part of me that my body and my conscious self didn't. There had to be more to my self than my thoughts and my physical appearance, and without realizing it, I was hungry to know that other part of myself. Unfortunately, at that time I didn't follow through on my vague awareness and attempt to discover what my shadow might actually represent.

In more recent years I learned how the unconscious can provide us with valuable emotional and spiritual information to help us live more fully. But what happens if we remain unaware of its promptings or choose to ignore them? We set the scene for conflict between our outer and inner self. We may feel tense, restless, insecure, moody, unsure of ourselves. The conflict may erupt as a physical ailment such as an ulcer, a skin rash, or colitis. An unexpressed feeling such as anger may burst forth unexpectedly, or a compulsive or forbidden behavior, which only causes us to work harder at holding the feeling down. It's as if there is another force in us, a dark, shadowy figure that tries to assert itself. In the song "Two Faces," Bruce Springsteen paints a vivid portrait of a man struggling with his unconscious or dark side:

> *Sometimes mister I feel sunny and wild*
> *Lord I love to see my baby smile*
> *Then dark clouds come rolling by*
> *Two faces have I*

One that laughs one that cries
One says hello one says goodbye
One does things I don't understand
Makes me feel like half a man

At night I get down on my knees and pray
Our love will make that other man go away
But he'll never say goodbye
Two faces have I[10]

That other man within us is the shadow. The unconscious indeed has many associations with a shadow: It is dark, indistinct, and mysterious. It can be sinister and evil at times, though it can also be good and beneficial to us. It always seems to be lurking over our shoulder, operating in some kind of parallel way to our conscious self. It appears to compensate in some way for our conscious thoughts and actions, just as a shadow grows larger when we move closer to a light source or gets darker as the light gets brighter.[11]

Many of us know that we have a dark side, but we can't figure out what to do with it. We usually assume that it is evil, intent on our destruction, and must be suppressed at all costs. Christians, perhaps, may be tempted to equate the shadow with our "sinful nature" and attempt to renounce it completely. What many people don't realize, however, is that our shadow side really wants to be our friend; that is, it wants to live in harmony with our conscious self. It doesn't want to be obeyed as much as it wants to be recognized, accepted, listened to. It has great emotional and spiritual wisdom to offer, and it attempts in a variety of ways to slip this information into our awareness. Dreams, daydreams, fantasies, imagination, creative expressions, unusual habits or interests or tastes, pet peeves, strong or sudden surges of emotion—these are only a few places we can look for signs of our shadow. It all depends on how interested we are in what it has to say. If we take the time to look and listen to its messages, our shadow will give us all kinds of opportunities for change and growth in our lives. But if we ignore or discount its voice, it will turn on us and make us miserable, much as it does to the man in the above song. And the more we avoid it, the more sinister and threatening and regressive it becomes.

Let me give a few examples. In literature, the most famous shadow image is that of Dr. Jekyll and Mr. Hyde in the story by Robert Louis Stevenson. Jekyll was the kind and civilized scientist, Hyde the evil murderer who was actually Jekyll's dark side. Even Jekyll's other name gives a clue to his shadow self: it's a part of him he wants to "hide."[12]

Well-known religious figures such as Jimmy Swaggart and Jim Bakker worked so hard to create a spiritual public image, one that somehow set them up as being above the ability to sin, that their shadow side had to compensate by getting them into trouble. In one of my former home towns, I knew a very conservative Christian man who had established a reputation as a Bible teacher and a staunch defender of fundamentalism. Once I happened to see him in the bleachers at a sports event, his face flushed with rage, viciously yelling that somebody should "kill the ref" for making a bad call. Someone told me that he always acted this way at ballgames. His shadow may have been trying to show him that he represses too much of his anger. Former Saturday morning TV star Pee Wee Herman almost never appeared in public as himself, Paul Reubens; he maintained his well-scrubbed, quirky, childish Pee Wee persona, even when appearing on talk shows. That seemed odd to me. When I heard of his arrest for masturbating in an X-rated theater, it occurred to me that perhaps his shadow simply could not tolerate being ignored.

The above examples portray the shadow as bad or evil, but the shadow can also hide good qualities that need to be brought into our conscious living. I think of a neighborhood kid that my son, Brendan, used to play with. This seven-year-old boy, who came from an abusive home, brought trouble wherever he went; within five minutes of his arrival, some kind of fight would break out. He kept up a tough-guy exterior and sometimes bullied other kids. When he and a dozen other children came over for Brendan's birthday party, I feared the worst as I quickly had to break up several altercations. A few minutes later, for one of the activities, I pretended I was Donald Duck and talked to the kids in a ducky voice. When this rough-and-tumble kid heard me, he immediately stopped his boisterous behavior, sat down and cuddled up next to me, asking "Donald" cute questions in a tender voice—to my utter amazement. He was much quieter and well-behaved for the rest of the party and asked for Donald several more times. I believe this boy's shadow was revealing a gentle child who wanted to love and be loved.

As I've sniffed around the corners of my consciousness, I've discovered parts of my shadow in a few unusual places: my musical tastes, for example. My compact-disc collection consists mainly of Irish folk musicians, singer-songwriters such as James Taylor and Paul Simon, and a stack of mellow Windham Hill artists. But there are other kinds of music I'm drawn to. I've already mentioned the period of time that I latched onto macho-female singers. In recent years I've been especially moved by certain male artists such as Bono of U2, Bruce Cockburn, Mike Scott of the Waterboys, Peter Gabriel, Van Morrison, and the musicians of Tears for Fears. The musical styles of these artists vary widely, but they all ignite my soul because of the incredible passion they embody in their performances. Their words and music come from deep within, whether they are songs about love, social injustice, God, or gut-wrenching pain. And they are performed with such intense emotion (honest emotion, not the fake showbiz gush) that I feel some part of myself being awakened as I listen. Somewhere in my shadow, that is, deep within myself, there is a powerful passion that longs to express itself as freely as these musicians do.

Another shadow discovery came when I stopped to ask myself why I am so fascinated by what I consider to be a violent sport: boxing. I've always been "officially" repulsed by the idea of two men beating each other's brains out. Yet when I'm scanning the TV channels with the remote control and I hit upon a boxing match, I always want to leave it on in the hope of seeing someone pounded into the mat. Why? Is my shadow trying to tell me something? I believe so. It's reminding me that there's a fighter or a warrior in me that needs to come out in some way. As a child I was discouraged from all fighting, so I sometimes got picked on, and never fought back, not even in self-defense. As an adult, when conflict arises I still find it hard to assert myself or to defend myself when I'm unfairly criticized. Oh, I may speak up or throw a few verbal punches, but then I quickly toss in the towel. My shadow wants to connect me with the inner warrior who knows how to be firm, forthright, and protective of my boundaries.

It is also possible to catch a glimpse of our shadow in the people and institutions we project it upon, if we are willing to be honest. For instance, I have an acute intolerance for people who make careless mistakes and machines that don't work properly. When I follow that disdain back to its source—in myself—I reluctantly have to confess my belief that I am all-too-often careless or that I fail to do what I'm supposed to be doing. I can even go one step deeper and recall the "careless" verdict given to me by my father. To make my own careless self feel better, I focus on the (supposed) ineptness of others. Another shadow projection I've discovered pertains to some of my colleagues in publishing. When I hear of writers who establish disciplined schedules and always meet their deadlines, I get suspicious. I find myself trying to discredit their work because (I tell myself) the deadline was more important to them than doing careful research, or some other lame excuse. But once again, if I look into myself, where the projector is running, I see someone who has always struggled with doing things on time, as far back as I can remember. (I was even late in delivering the manuscript for this book.) I also have to admit my own tendency to be perfectionistic and my inability to let go and trust myself to do a job well.

Just as we store positive as well as negative qualities in our shadow, we can also project positive qualities on others, not realizing that they are buried parts of ourselves. Robert A. Johnson writes:

> It is possible to project from the shadow the very best of oneself onto another person or situation. Our hero-worshiping capacity is pure shadow; in this case our finest qualities are refused and laid on another. It is hard to understand, but we often refuse to bear our noble traits and instead find a shadow substitute for them.[13]

Projection of the shadow can also occur at the group or cultural level. Fundamentalists brand theological liberals as heretics, apostates, and non-Christians in order to compensate for their own failures in the area of social concern and open-mindedness. Liberals stereotype fundamentalists (and many evangelicals) as mindless, bigoted hillbillies so as to avoid facing their own need to encounter God personally. Sadaam Hussein and George Bush could not find workable solutions to their countries' internal problems, so they attempted to unite their peoples around an outside enemy. Bush became the Great Satan and Hussein a ruthless barbarian.

Why all this talk about the shadow and the unconscious? Because it is part of us, and if we are to become whole and balanced men, we need to integrate its riches, and even its darkness, into our conscious life. I'm not saying that we need to become more sinister persons or that we should do one raunchy thing every week for our health's sake. Rather, we need to recognize and accept the dark part of ourselves, the part that has the capacity to do some pretty awful things.

A number of years ago, while chatting with a woman after church, I casually mentioned that I went to a psychotherapist. "You do?" she gasped in horror. "Oh, I would never do that! People would think I was crazy!" I was struck by the intensity of her response. Less than two years after that conversation, she left her husband without warning and ran off with a married man. This woman appeared to be terrified of her own dark side and attempted to extinguish it completely, only to find out that it had gotten the best of her. But suppose she had been able to say to herself, "Yes, there is a part of me that could be tempted by another man, and that scares me. Maybe it's worth taking a closer look at myself and my marriage." By looking into her shadow, she could have taken a step toward growth and wholeness.

Whether we like it or not, our shadow will overpower us if we don't acknowledge and accept its presence. While it may sound easy to do, it often involves a great deal of inner struggle to recognize the forces at work in us, both good and evil. In the New Testament, the apostle Paul was extremely aware of the war within:

> I do not understand what I do. For what I want to do I do not do, but what I hate I do. . . . For I have the desire to do what is good, but I cannot carry it out. For what I do is not the good I want to do; no, the evil I do not want to do—this I keep on doing. Now if I do what I do not want to do, it is no longer I who do it, but it is sin living in me that does it. So I find this law at work: When I want to do good, evil is right there with me. For in my inner being I delight in God's law. . . . (Romans 7:15, 18–22).

Some people feel that Paul in this passage was talking about life before his conversion to Christianity or about some "backslidden" state. But I believe he was describing the way life really is. Like Paul, we must accept the presence of both good and evil in ourselves, and no matter what we do, we cannot get rid of the evil. Only by acknowledging the evil within and understanding how it works can we truly and actively choose the good, or, as in Paul's case, can we choose to turn our lives over to God.

A line of dialogue in the movie *Backdraft* provides insight into the way we can approach our shadow. A rookie firefighter, Brian McCaffrey (played by William Baldwin), assists in investigating a series of suspicious fires, and becomes a student of the chief investigator of the fire department, Donald Rimgale (Robert De Niro). At one point, the two men are examining the charred remains of a building, and Rimgale talks about the nature of fire: "It's a living thing, Brian. It breathes, it eats—and it hates. The only way to beat it is to think like it. . . . Some guys on this job, fire owns 'em. It makes 'em fight it on its level. But the only way to truly kill it is to love it a little." Our shadow self operates in a similar way. When we ignore it or repress it, it eats away at us, sapping our energy and draining our creativity. The shadow hates too, but the kind of things it hates are dishonesty, denial of feelings and desires, refusal to face fears. If we aren't willing to look into its darkness, then it will turn on us, "own" us, move in some negative way to assert itself. It simply must be recognized, but even more, it needs to be accepted, even loved, so that its power and wisdom can become a part of our conscious life.

Sometimes we even need to sit down and face our shadow directly. In a recent edition of *60 Minutes,* reporter Leslie Stahl spoke with several FBI agents whose job was to interview jailed serial killers for hours at a time, asking them to describe every gruesome detail of their heinous crimes. The agents' purpose? To get inside the minds of these murderers and understand their motives, patterns, and methods, so that other killers who are still at large can be apprehended. In the same way, we can "interview" the "criminals" in ourselves to keep them in check.

I want to emphasize again that the voices from our shadow or unconscious do not have to be enemy voices. They can be voices of encouragement, of affirmation, of challenge, of warning. But whatever they are, paying attention to them will make a major difference in the lives of passive men. The shadow wants to keep us honest, as honest as we can possibly be with ourselves. It wants us to be balanced and whole.

How is all this inner searching going to help us as passive men? First, we will learn more about who we are, what our deepest needs and desires are, what areas of life we need to work on. We can use this information to make our own active choices based on the deeper wisdom within us, rather than passively depending on others.

Second, we can find within our shadow the missing pieces of our masculinity, if we are willing to hunt and fish for them. I will take a closer look at some of these pieces in the final chapter.

Third, we will likely feel more energy for living, because it takes a lot of energy to repress our feelings and resist the promptings of our deeper self. By allowing the trapdoor to open rather than constantly trying to hold it down, we can put the energy we've saved to a positive, creative use.

Fourth, by acknowledging our inner self, with all its conflicting elements—good and evil, male and female, child and adult—we learn to accept and love ourselves. When I listen to the voice within, I find myself drawing closer to the core of who I am—my true identity. There is greater harmony between my outer and my inner being; I feel more at peace with myself, more at one with myself.

Finally, listening to our unconscious will bring us nearer to God. "The kingdom of God is within you," Jesus said (Luke 17:21). Since God dwells within us by his Holy Spirit, we can best commune with him through our own spirit or soul, that is, our unconscious. The deeper we can plumb our soul and tap its riches, the more we become truly ourselves, and the more we can experience God's presence and think his thoughts. Listen to how David describes God's relationship to his inner person in Psalm 139:

> *O LORD, you have searched me*
> *and you know me.*
> *You know when I sit and when I rise;*
> *you perceive my thoughts from afar. . . .*
> *Before a word is on my tongue*
> *you know it completely, O LORD. . . .*
> *Where can I go from your Spirit?*
> *Where can I flee from your presence?*
> *If I go up to the heavens, you are there;*
> *if I make my bed in the depths, you are there. . . .*
> *If I say, "Surely the darkness will hide me*
> *and the light become night around me,"*
> *even the darkness will not be dark to you;*
> *the night will shine like the day,*
> *for darkness is as light to you.*
> *For you created my inmost being;*
> *you knit me together in my mother's womb.*
> *I praise you because I am fearfully and wonderfully made;*
> *your works are wonderful,*
> *I know that full well. . . .*
> *How precious to me are your thoughts, O God!*
> *How vast is the sum of them!*
> *Were I to count them,*
> *they would outnumber the grains of sand.*
> *When I awake,*
> *I am still with you. . . .*
> *Search me, O God, and know my heart;*
> *test me and know my anxious thoughts.*
> *See if there is any offensive way in me,*
> *and lead me in the way everlasting.*

It really is possible for us as men to have this kind of intimacy, this kind of communion, with our inner selves and with God. It's all there deep inside of us, underneath the trapdoor, waiting to be found. And as we travel inward to find it, we'll discover that it's not an "it" at all, but rather an "I"—the "I" of our true male identity, and the "I AM" of the person of God dwelling within us.

Six

The Myth-ing Link

A man is always a teller of tales; he lives surrounded by his stories and the stories of others; he sees everything that happens to him through them; and he tries to live his own life as if he were telling a story.

—*Jean-Paul Sartre*

When I first began reading about the men's movement, I found myself saying, "Okay, I see the psychological value of a man working things out with his father, getting together with other men, and learning to look inward. But why all the mythology and fairy tales? What does that have to do with masculinity?"

Then I picked up *Iron John,* and as I saw how Robert Bly explored this Grimm fairy tale as a road map for developing mature masculinity, I experienced for myself the power and relevance of its truths, which seemed not to be imposed on the story, but rather to bubble up from within it. Then I read the narrative of Parsifal and his search for the Holy Grail, as illuminated by Robert A. Johnson in the book *HE: Understanding Masculine Psychology.* Again I encountered deep truths that seemed to transcend culture and time, and yet relate to me personally. I also listened to tapes of Bly and Michael Meade talking about tales such as "The Firebird," "The Devil's Sooty Brother," and "The Water of Life." While these fairy tales had a masculine tone, others I read seemed to be more feminine and spoke in a unique way to the souls of women. But after reading and listening to a number of these stories (and reflecting on others I'd already read), I felt my deeper self being awakened and nourished. What was it about these myths and tales?

BYPASSING THE BRAIN

In chapter 3 I briefly mentioned the part that mythology plays in the men's movement. Here I'd like to look a little more closely at how myth works and explore a few ways that men can become involved with stories and experience some of their guiding and healing power. By myths and fairy tales I am not referring to our culture's popular understanding of those terms, that is, that myths are falsehoods, disproven theories, or mere archaeological curiosities. Nor am I talking about children's books or fiction in general. Mother Goose, Hans Christian Andersen, and other modernized versions of ancient tales that moralize or remove all the violence and pain do not qualify either.

I am speaking of the oldest stories that have endured for centuries such as those collected by the brothers Grimm, and others that have been occasionally retold creatively and faithfully by present-day writers. For instance, in his novel *Ulysses,* James Joyce retold the ancient story of the Greek hero Odysseus, but Joyce set the scene in turn-of-the-century Dublin. Some Christian writers have been fascinated with recycling ancient myths. George MacDonald reworked old Hebrew myths in his fantasy novel *Lilith.* C. S. Lewis drew from the tales of Arthur and the Knights of the Round Table for his novel *That Hideous Strength,* and in his famous *Chronicles of Narnia* he borrowed heavily from a wide variety of mythic sources: animal fables, fairy tales, Middle Eastern folktales, and Norse mythology. And even J. R. R. Tolkien leaned heavily on Norse and Celtic mythology in creating his popular *Lord of the Rings.*

Myths and fairy tales such as these connect us to a deeper, fuller reality as we read them and experience them. Their images and symbols reveal the world as it really is, the way we "know" it is deep inside us, but have somehow forgotten in our everyday life. There is an order and unity about them that challenges us to find order and purpose in our own lives. Often the central character in these stories— the hero—is on some kind of journey or quest, and if we look carefully, we can see ourselves in the trials he must undergo. While these stories speak to all human beings, male and female, I see now why they may have a special value to today's men—in particular passive men. We are so used to doing all our living with our heads, trying to think our way out of our problems, coming up with systems and facts and answers, all the while denying the deeper wisdom, the deeper reality, the deeper feeling within us. We need all the help we can get to access those other parts of ourselves. Myths and fairy tales bypass our intellectualizing and travel right to the heart, via the imagination. Christian scholar and apologist C. S. Lewis put it this way:

> [Myth] goes beyond the expression of things we have already felt. It arouses in us sensations we have never had before, never anticipated having, as though we had broken out of our normal mode of consciousness. . . . It gets under our skin, hits us at a deeper level than our thoughts or even our passions, troubles oldest certainties till all questions are re-opened, and in general shocks us more fully awake than we are for most of our lives.[1]

To be out of touch with one's deeper self, one's male identity, one's purpose for living, is to be asleep. That is why passive men need to be "shocked awake" more often. And getting involved with some of these ancient stories is the way to do it. "Myth is the name of a way of seeing, a way of knowing in depth, a way of experiencing," said the late Clyde Kilby, who taught modern mythology at Wheaton College in Illinois. "Myth is a lane down which we walk in order to repossess our soul."[2] P. L. Travers, creator of *Mary Poppins,* explains how myth and identity are so related:

> Perhaps the myths are telling us that [the hero's] endeavors are not so much voyages of discovery as of rediscovery; that the hero is seeking not for something new but for something old, a treasure that was lost and has to be found, his own self, his identity. And by finding this, by achieving this, he takes part in the one task, the

essential mythical requirement: the reinstatement of the fallen world.³

The great myths and tales are much more than good stories that help us get in touch with our feelings. They invite us to embark on a journey to the center of ourselves, where we can discover not only who we are, but also how we can make a difference in the world. This is true for both men and women, but I think so many men today have lost contact with their center that they stand to benefit in a special way from these stories.

So how should men read a myth or fairy tale, and how do we figure out what it means? Someone once asked George MacDonald this question, and he responded, "It is there not so much to convey a meaning as to wake a meaning." Fairy tales, he said, are designed "not to give [someone] things to think about, but to wake things up that are in him . . . to make him think for himself." He suggests that we listen to fairy tales the same way we listen to music, "not to bring the forces of our intellect to bear upon it, but to be still and let it work on that part of us for whose sake it exists."⁴

MYTH AND THE BIBLE

At this point, Christians may say, "Why should I bother with all these myths and tales when I can read the Bible? Doesn't it tell me what I need in order to be a man?" Yes it does, and much more; but the Bible is also a great place to begin reading mythology. Let me explain. Christians believe that the Bible is historically true, that the events in the Bible really happened. So do I, since I too am a Christian. But I also believe that the Bible can be read as story—as mythology. Not only is the Bible true historically, but it is also true mythologically—that is, it contains all the characteristics of myth which I've described above. I'm not suggesting that we stop reading it as fact; the central doctrines and principles of Scripture are extremely important for our life and growth. What I am suggesting is that Christians (and everyone!) can greatly benefit by reading it both as fact and as story or myth.

C. S. Lewis affirms both the factual and the mythical value of the Bible as follows:

> The heart of Christianity is a myth which is also a fact. The old myth of the Dying God, *without ceasing to be* myth, comes down from the heaven of legend and imagination to the earth of history. It *happens*—at a particular date, in a particular place, followed by definable historical consequences. . . . By becoming fact it does not cease to be myth; that is the miracle. . . . To be truly Christian we must both assent to the historical fact and also receive the myth (fact though it has become) with the same imaginative embrace which we accord to all myths. The one is hardly more necessary than the other.[5]

Though God has always been around, Christianity hasn't. And yet the Bible says that "what may be known about God is plain" to all humankind, "because God made it plain to them" (Romans 1:19). How did God do this? Most certainly through nature, but I believe, with Lewis and Tolkien, that he also make himself known by scattering stories around the world. While the stories have different settings and characters, and may have been modified by various cultures over the centuries, many of them have striking parallels. They speak of divine beings who created the world, how they took the initiative to come down into that world and make contact with the people, and how they showed humans how to relate to each other and to God. Though these myths, legends, and folk tales are not Christian truth, perhaps they were one of God's ways of preparing the world for the coming of Christ.

But the stories also have value on their own as a useful framework for living, then and now. Many feature a hero who must undergo a series of trials and ordeals to reach his goal. The variety of these stories, their beauty, their terror, their unusual details and twists, are all designed by God to convey truth (at another level) about the way the world works. We experience a special kind of wisdom in these stories that we rarely pick up from our parents or from schools—valuable clues on how to cope with life's transitions and challenges. Usually the clues speak to the inner world of the psyche or the self.

We can experience and enjoy many of the biblical stories in the same way we can these other ancient tales, if we allow ourselves to read them as myth in addition to seeing them as fact.

For example, we can read the biblical story of Jacob and Esau as a historical account of two brothers, one a conniving Mama's boy and the other a tough, hairy Papa's kid. We can observe their actions and the lessons they learned and extract principles about serving God and following his covenant and making up with one's estranged brother. All of this is completely legitimate. But in addition to seeing this as a historical narrative, we can give the passage a mythological reading. In doing this, we see a picture of two opposing sides of ourselves—an "inner" Jacob and an "inner" Esau—that somehow need to be reconciled. The experiences Jacob has, such as dreaming, wrestling with the angel, and so on, parallel events that need to occur within ourselves. I am not talking about exchanging one kind of interpretation of the Bible for another; I am suggesting that there are numerous layers of truth and unspeakable riches in the many stories of Scripture, if Christians will open themselves to these other dimensions.

Ministers and priests try to uncover these deeper levels every Sunday in their sermons; they help us to internalize the stories of the Bible. Unfortunately, many of them don't go far enough. Some ignore the Bible's stories and focus primarily on doctrinal teachings. Others may examine the stories, but only at the intellectual level, to extract propositions and principles. Or they may clean up the grittiness and use the stories to promote white middle-class values. The great preachers, however, incorporate both the factual truth and the mythological truth of the biblical narratives.

The "dying god" myth that C. S. Lewis speaks of is one of the finest examples of the mythological dimension, one that has special significance for Christians. He continues:

> Those who do not know that this great myth [of the dying god] became Fact when the Virgin conceived are, indeed, to be pitied. But Christians also need to be reminded . . . that what became Fact was a Myth, that it carries with it into the world of Fact all the properties of a myth. . . . We must not be ashamed of the mythical radiance resting on our theology. We must not be nervous about "parallels" and "Pagan Christs": they *ought* to be there—it would be a stumbling block if they weren't. We must not, in false spirituality, withhold our imaginative welcome. If God chooses to be mythopoeic—and is not the sky itself a myth—shall we refuse to be *mythopathic*? For this is the marriage of heaven and earth: Perfect Myth and Perfect Fact: claiming not only our love and our obedience, but also our wonder and delight, addressed to the savage, the child, and the poet in each one of us no less than to the moralist, the scholar, and the philosopher.[6]

J. R. R. Tolkien, who was also a Christian and a close friend of C. S. Lewis, gives a glimpse of the deeper joy we can feel when we appreciate the Bible's mythical dimension as well as its historicity. He says that many fairy stories contain turning points that are both wonderful and cataclysmic at the same time. The name he gives to these turning points is "eucatastrophe," meaning a "good catastrophe" that ultimately leads to the story's happy ending. The biblical account of Christ is a prime example of a fairy tale's power:

> The Gospels contain a fairy-story, or a story of a larger kind which embraces all the essence of fairy-stories. They

contain many marvels—peculiarly artistic, beautiful, and moving: "mythical" in their perfect, self-contained significance; and among the marvels is the greatest and most complete conceivable eucatastrophe. But this story has entered History and the primary world. . . . The Birth of Christ is the eucatastrophe of Man's history. The Resurrection is the eucatastrophe of the story of the Incarnation. This story begins and ends in joy. It has pre-eminently the "inner consistency of reality." There is no tale ever told that men would rather find was true, and none which so many sceptical men have accepted as true on its own merits. For the Art of it has the supremely convincing tone of Primary Art, that is, of Creation. To reject it leads either to sadness or to wrath. . . . But this story is supreme; and it is true. Art has been verified. God is the Lord, or angels, and of men—and of elves. Legend and History have met and fused.[7]

Those who do not believe in the historicity of the Bible can still partake of its riches at the mythological level, because it speaks not only to the intellect, but to the imagination and the unconscious "deeper self" passive men are trying to discover. "Myth is necessary because reality is so much larger than rationality," Clyde Kilby has said. "Not that myth is irrational but that it easily accommodates the rational while rising above it."[8] His words apply not only to myth in general, but to the mythological dimension of the Bible.

THE STORY OF MY LIFE

So far I've tried to establish the value of reading myths, legends, and fairy tales, including the stories in the Bible, as a way for passive men to reconnect with their deeper identity. For the Christian reader, I've tried to show that the Bible can legitimately be read as myth and fact.

But there is another way that these stories can speak to us: They remind us that our own lives are a story and that we can examine the people and events in our own story as a way of finding out who we are. Because our culture has lost its appreciation for myths and fairy tales in general, it has also lost sight of the reality that each of our lives is a story, a sacred story.

We all have a built-in appreciation for stories. In fact, I think we even have a built-in ability to discern a great story from a mediocre or bad one. We use this ability every time we watch a movie, for instance. When we leave the theater or rewind the videotape, we instinctively know what made the movie "work" or not. The hero wasn't believable enough because his victory over the bad guy came too easily. Or all the action was external with no inner character growth—speeding the pulse but not stirring the soul. Or conversely, the movie was satisfying or honest or real because the main character achieved victory not only over the bad guy, but over the dark and fearful part of himself, and that victory came through great struggle and growth.

You'll recall that in the best stories, certain key moments arise in the hero's life where he must make choices—choices upon which the entire outcome of the story depends. They may involve choosing between an old pattern of living and a new one, between what others expect of him and what he truly desires in his soul, between doing nothing and "doing the right thing," between temporary pleasure and long-term fulfillment, between the practical and the meaningful, between temporal and eternal values, between the safe option and the dangerous but ultimately more satisfying one. And the degree to which a character turns out to be a hero depends on how he handles these choices. Does he face them directly or attempt to avoid them altogether? Does he look to someone else to make a choice for him? Does he make the right choice merely by chance or by a conscious decision? Does he make the choice not just with his head, but with his full self, and does the choice show in his life and his actions? Do the choices bring about a fundamental change in his character, so that he is a deeper, wiser, more alive person afterward?

These are the questions we ask intuitively of fictional characters we encounter in books and movies. But we can ask the very same questions of our own lives as the leading characters in our own stories. The answers can give us much insight into how heroic a life we have been living, as well as guidance into what choices lie ahead and what choices we need to be making. All of these questions and answers and choices can contribute to our process of finding and reclaiming our identity as men.

There's a wonderful passage in Tolkien's *Lord of the Rings* that illustrates the importance of accepting one's own story and living it out in a responsible way. Let's take a few minutes to enter into this story and see what it has to say to us. The epic chronicles the adventures of Frodo Baggins, a "hobbit" who has been entrusted with a powerful ring that he must protect from the evil Sauron, who intends to use it to destroy all freedom and goodness. Frodo's journey is not without many perils. At one point in the story, Frodo and his loyal friend, Sam, are talking about all the danger and trouble they've had to go through.

> "But so our path is laid." [Frodo said.]
> "Yes, that's so," said Sam. "And we shouldn't be here at all, if we'd known more about it before we started. But I suppose it's often that way. The brave things in the old tales and songs, Mr. Frodo: adventures, as I used to call them. I used to think that they were things the wonderful folk of the stories went out and looked for, because they wanted them, because they were exciting and life was a bit dull, a kind of sport, as you might say. But that's not the way of it with the tales that really mattered, or the ones that stay in the mind. Folk seem to have been just landed in them usually—their paths were laid that way, as you put it. But I expect they had lots of chances, like us, of turning back, only they didn't. And if they had, we shouldn't know, because they'd have been forgotten. We

hear about those as just went on—and not at all to a good
end, mind you; at least not to what folk inside a story and
not outside it call a good end. You know, coming home
and finding things all right, though not quite the same—
like old Mr. Bilbo. But those aren't always the best tales
to hear, though they may be the best tales to get landed
in! I wonder what sort of tale we've fallen into?"

"I wonder," said Frodo. "But I don't know. And that's
the way of a real tale. Take any one that you're fond of.
You may know, or guess, what kind of a tale it is, happy-
ending or sad-ending, but the people in it don't know.
And you don't want them to."

"No sir, of course not. Beren now, he never thought
he was going to get the Silmaril from the Iron Crown in
Thangorodrim, and yet he did, and that was a worse place
and a blacker danger than ours. But that's a long tale, of
course, and goes on past the happiness and into grief and
beyond it—and the Silmaril went on and came to
Earendil. And why, sir, I never thought of that before!
We've got—you've got some of the light of it in that star-
glass that the Lady gave you! Why, to think of it, we're in
the same tale still! It's going on. Don't the great tales
never end?"

"No, they never end as tales," said Frodo. "But the
people in them come, and go when their part's ended.
Our part will end later—or sooner."

"And then we can have some rest and some sleep,"
said Sam. He laughed grimly. "And I mean just that, Mr.
Frodo. I mean plain ordinary rest, and sleep, and waking
up to a morning's work in the garden. I'm afraid that's all
I'm hoping for all the time. All the big important plans are
not for my sort. Still I wonder if we shall ever be put into
songs or tales. We're in one, of course; but I mean, put
into words, you know, told by the fireside, or read out of a
great big book with red and black letters, years and years
afterwards. And people will say: 'Let's hear about Frodo
and the Ring!' And they'll say: 'Yes, that's one of my
favourite stories. Frodo was very brave, wasn't he, dad?'
'Yes, my boy, the famousest of the hobbits, and that's
saying a lot.'"

"It's saying a lot too much," said Frodo, and he laughed, a long clear laugh from his heart. Such a sound had not been heard in those places since Sauron came to Middle-earth. To Sam suddenly it seemed as if all the stones were listening and the tall rocks leaning over them. But Frodo did not heed them; he laughed again. "Why, Sam," he said, "to hear you somehow makes me as merry as if the story was already written."9

In this scene, Frodo and Sam do something that all men (indeed, all people) would benefit from doing: they stand back and look at how their lives are a story, and how their life-stories have been woven into a much larger, grander tale. It is just this kind of reflection and awareness that gives them a clearer sense of their identity as men—well, hobbits. And because of this awareness, they become active participants in their stories rather than passive observers, or worse, helpless victims.

As I listened to the conversation between Frodo and Sam, I found myself disagreeing at first with Sam's conclusion that people "just landed in" their stories. It seemed too deterministic to me, too beyond our free will to choose the life we live. But then it occurred to me that I "landed in" the middle of a story just by being born. I landed in a certain family headed up by two parents who had a certain kind of background that they carried into my story. (For some, one or both of these parents may not even be present, physically or emotionally.) My family had a middle-class economic status that gave me access to some experiences and denied me access to others. I landed in a particular state and country, a particular culture, at a particular time in history. I didn't choose any of these things, and yet I don't feel my life has been totally determined by God or fate. It's more a matter of choosing to accept the kind of life—the story—I was born into.

As I came to that conclusion, Sam's follow-up comment made more sense: "I expect they had lots of chances, like us, of turning back, only they didn't." Or as the saying goes, "You've got to play the hand that's dealt you."

Three kinds of stories are mentioned in the course of this conversation: what literary scholars would call, technically, *myth, monomyth,* and *mythopoeia,* which (for our purposes) stand for Our Own Story, The Great Story, and The Written Story.[10] All three play a vital part in helping a man (indeed, anyone) discover and take hold of his identity. Frodo and Sam were able to distinguish between them. Taking the last one first, mythopoeia refers to all the stories ("the tales that really mattered," according to Sam) that have been captured and recorded in written form, as legends, tales, songs, poems, plays, and art. As we experience these written stories, we somehow see ourselves more clearly. (The branch of the men's movement I have focused upon in this book is often called the "mythopoetic" branch.) The monomyth is the "one story" of the world's creation, fall, and redemption, the grand plot which all other myths mirror or participate in. And at the personal level, a myth represents one's own life story, with its wounds, goals, trials, setbacks, and triumphs.

It's extremely difficult to understand a literary character fully—where he came from, the forces that affected his life, how he faced challenges—without observing him in a story. In the same way, we men cannot understand ourselves unless we know our own stories.

God has given us the ability to stand back from and evaluate our own lives—our own stories—in the same way the hobbits Frodo and Sam did above. It is this kind of self-evaluating, self-listening exercise that can help us get a clearer picture of who we are and how we fit into God's plan for the world. By listening to our own stories, we can learn to distinguish between our two "selves"—the self we project for the world to see and the deeper, truer self we are carrying around inside us. These two selves are usually quite different from each other, but as we become more aware of and learn to honor that deeper, inner self, we will find our outer self becoming more authentic. We will feel a greater sense of inner harmony. We will feel more whole. We will have a stronger grasp on our identity. And we will be able to live more actively, more consciously.

Here are a few questions we can ask ourselves to begin with: What's the overall plot of my story so far? What are the key people and events of my life? What are the strongest forces that have guided my life? What have been the major turning points in my life, and how did they change the direction of my story? Which of these turning points were thrust upon me, and which did I choose? What kind of quest or journey am I participating in? If I were to parallel my life with that of a mythical or historical hero, at what point would I be in my story? What do I like and dislike about the story I've been living? Is the story I have lived so far believable? Does it ring true? If so, what has made it that way? If not, what is needed to make my story more authentic? Is there some kind of risk or step I need to take, a challenge or struggle I need to meet, a dark or ugly part of myself or my past that I need to face? Is there a voice within me, calling to me out of my deepest yearnings like the voice that spoke to Ray Kinsella (played by Kevin Costner) in *Field of Dreams?*

Christian writer and philosopher Mircea Eliade has written that "myths describe the various and sometimes dramatic breakthroughs of the sacred (or the 'supernatural') into the World."[11] As we look back over our own myth or life story, it would be valuable to ask: Have there been times, perhaps only moments, when the sacred, or God, "broke through" into my life? Are there experiences I can recall in which the effects on me were larger and more profound than any human effort could have brought about? Have I dismissed those moments as mere coincidence, or have I embraced them as part of a greater Purpose in my life? Perhaps it's worth taking a second look at the painful experiences too, the ones that gave us wounds or caused us to suffer. We could ask ourselves, Did that wound or that pain alter my life in a way that eventually turned out to be positive and growth-producing? Did it ultimately cause me to embark on the journey toward wholeness that I am now traveling? Would I be where I am today—seeking a deeper, more fulfilling, more meaningful life—if it were not for that pain? Is it possible, then, that God could have broken into my life *through* my pain—not as the author of the suffering but as the one who used it to propel my life, my self, toward wholeness?

About ten years ago, I went through a particularly difficult time of life. My first marriage was unhappy, and I was encountering a great deal of stress in my job. I felt like a victim—stuck and paralyzed, unable to do anything to fix my problems. But one night, as I lay alone in bed, something happened to me. I can't remember if I was awake or asleep, but I felt a loving, reassuring Presence around me and in me. Wordlessly this Presence, which I took to be God, communicated a simple message to me: *I am with you. I am in control. I see the bigger picture.* That was all. The brief experience of this Presence was so powerful and so encouraging that my entire body relaxed that night, and with it my spirit.

I suppose this encounter could have led me to say, "Oh good—God's gonna step in and fix my life for me." But for some reason it didn't. There had been no flashes of light, no answers to my questions, no solutions to my problems. Only God's presence. To my surprise, in the weeks and months that followed, I felt a greater sense of my own power to change my life. Somehow, knowing that God was a part of my story caused me to take more responsibility for myself, to make more active choices. The marriage ultimately failed, but it was not the end; my growth continued, slowly but surely. Today my life is so much richer than before, not because of that one divine encounter, but because of hundreds of holy epiphanies in my life that occur sometimes through silence, sometimes through events, and sometimes through other people. They are all parts of my story, and they all contribute to who I am.

By piecing together the myth of our own life, by coming to understand our own story, we not only gain a clearer sense of our identity, but we also come to realize that we are the author of that story, and that we have the power to direct its main character and change the story's plot to fit the desires and longings of our deepest, wisest self. Like the hobbits in *Lord of the Rings,* however, we also need to remember that our story is part of a much larger Story, one that is beyond our control and that will continue long after we're gone. At times we may find ourselves being cast as a participant in that grander Story, and we will have to choose whether to accept the part. The great myths and fairy tales show us that as we listen to and follow the Author's call, we will not only discover our identity and learn to live an active, conscious life, but we will contribute to the redemption of the world.

Seven

Living on Purpose

The heroic quest ... is first about taking a journey to find the treasure of your true self, and then about returning home to give your gift to help transform the kingdom—and, in the process, your own life.

—*Carol S. Pearon*

W *e have seen* that myths and fairy tales can help passive men by shedding light on the path that will lead us toward maturity and wholeness. They can also help by reminding us that our own lives are a story and that we can make active choices to affect its outcome. Yet another dimension of myth, which can have very practical application in our lives, is the rich imagery of *archetypes*.

An archetype is a universal symbol that has carried certain meanings and associations throughout history and across cultures. I've already given the example of water as a symbol of birth, new life, cleansing, and the unconscious—a symbol that appears not only in the Bible but also throughout world myths and literature. The image of wind can represent the breath of life, the spirit, or inspiration. A circle or sphere can stand for wholeness or unity. In the church, we see archetypes such as the cross, bread, wine, blood, and many others. There are thousands of these images and a host of associations. Most of these meanings linger in the unconscious, but if we recognize them (in stories and in our dreams, for instance) and make them conscious, they will awaken us from our passivity and nourish our souls.

Robert Moore and Douglas Gillette have pioneered research into various archetypes that specifically pertain to masculinity. Their findings, many of which I've relied upon in this chapter, appear in the groundbreaking work *King, Warrior, Magician, Lover*.[1] Moore and Gillette see these four archetypes as essential to the "mature masculine" self.

Robert Bly talks about another archetype, the Wild Man, in
Iron John. While all of these archetypes are extremely
important (and even these are not the only ones useful to
men), in this final chapter I want to explore in more depth
the three archetypes that have special significance for *passive*
men: the Wild Man, the Warrior, and the King.

I enter into this area with a keen awareness that I am
teetering on the outer edges of my own growth. While I can
appreciate the fullness of these images and their value to my
life, I am only beginning the process of awakening them
within myself. But the first step toward bringing these parts
of ourselves to life is recognizing that they are there and
learning to honor them. By looking more closely at my own
relationship to these inner beings, and how they can
complete the missing parts of my masculinity, I hope I will
encourage other passive men to do the same.

THE WILD SIDE

Energy, intensity, spontaneity, and fierceness are a few
words that characterize a man who is in touch with his inner
Wild Man. He feels alive, involved in and connected to the
world. He wants to taste a variety of experiences and feel
the full range of his feelings. We feel more of our wildness
as children, but in today's society that kind of exuberance is
often discouraged, and by the time we reach adulthood we
have learned to take the path of predictability and safety.

Over the course of our lives, however, we occasionally
feel the need to leave that path for a moment and do
something outlandish, something that reminds us that we
were not created solely for the purpose of sitting behind a
desk or operating the same piece of machinery every day.
We may want to go whitewater rafting or scuba diving or
travel on a whim to some exotic destination. These urges, I
believe, come from the Wild Man part of us.

For many Christians, this aspect of the Wild Man simply

means, "Loosen up, live a little." In spite of the illustrations we've seen of "gentle Jesus, meek and mild," the New Testament gives anything but this one-sided portrait. Sure, he welcomed the little children, but he also rode boats in the middle of storms, whipped people and threw them out of the temple, screamed in outrage at evil and hypocrisy, wept openly in public, went to gala events such as weddings and parties, and was accused of being a glutton and a drunkard. Jesus did all these things, and yet the Bible states that he never sinned. In other words, he lived fully, out of the complete range of his emotions. He followed his instincts.

A number of years ago my friend Jim called me on a Thursday night. His brother played for a college football team outside of Nashville and had a home game on Saturday. Jim had gotten this crazy idea that he and I could leave our home in suburban Chicago after work on Friday, drive all night and go to the game on Saturday, then leave first thing Sunday morning and be back home by evening. I agreed that it was a crazy idea, but I also knew it would be a great way to break my routine and have some fun, so I said yes. We had a fabulous time, and I have often told myself I should do something like that more frequently. By allowing myself to be spontaneous, I experienced the part of me that was more than a 9-to-5 employee who mowed the lawn on weekends.

While we can't always drop everything and vanish for a weekend, we can make ourselves more aware of these wild urges and find ways to build them into our lives. To dismiss them or reject them as youthful fantasies is to deny a real part of ourselves. One way I feed my denial is by envying others who get out and try new things or who take time to really enjoy themselves. I say to myself, "Too bad I can't do that." But why can't I?

Another Wild Man characteristic is the element of risk.

As a child, I recall flying down a steep hill on my bike and careening over a makeshift ramp that would send me ten feet into the air before I slammed into the ground. I would laugh, pick myself up, and do it again—sometimes with another guy on my bike. I thought I was Evel Knievel. Or when my family went camping in the mountains, I'd scramble effortlessly over the rocks, leaping from point to point, trying to reach the outermost cliff. I didn't stop to think, "Hmm, I could die if I slipped and fell." My parents, of course, panicked.

Along with many other men, I believed that once I reached adulthood—which amounted to getting married—I had to give up doing wild or crazy or unusual things. As an adult, I don't really need to pirouette across rock formations, but I do need to be willing to take risks. The Wild Man reminds us that doing what is safest, what is expected, or what is most acceptable to our family or community is not necessarily the way to live a life of meaning and purpose. I have a long way to go to integrate my Wild Man, but several experiences over the years have kept him alive in me. In the mid-1970s (back when there was an Iron Curtain), I traveled with some friends into Czechoslovakia and Hungary to visit Christians and their churches. On one occasion we were detained and questioned at the border; on another we were followed and stopped by police. In the early 1980s I interviewed the leader of a white-supremacist group for a magazine article, and during the course of my visit was accused of spying. Just a couple of years ago, after living every minute of my life in the suburbs, I moved with Nancy into downtown Chicago. (A job change for Nancy prompted us to leave fourteen months later, but we both agreed that we'd move back if we could.) These experiences all represented risks for me, but they gave me a broader perspective on life and put me in touch with deeper parts of myself. My life would not be as rich had I not taken those risks.

The Wild Man also embodies fierceness, which is not savagery, but rather action that is forthright, full of conviction, engaging body, mind, and emotions. I have found this trait to be hideously lacking in myself; I can recall no models of healthy fierceness in my past. I'm aware, with many others, of rage and violence in men, but not true fierceness. In the Old Testament, Samson, Saul, and David showed fierceness at times, as did John the Baptist and the disciple Peter in the New Testament. Even Jesus demonstrated a fierce, forthright attitude in many of his encounters with the Pharisees. Not surprisingly, his power and conviction struck fear into his followers and enemies alike. Wild Man energy can have this effect at times. Jesus was called "the Lion of Judah" in Old Testament prophecy. And when C. S. Lewis wanted to depict God in his *Chronicles of Narnia,* he chose a lion, Aslan, who in the story was wonderfully good and terrifying at the same time.

In the movie *City Slickers,* three men decide to deal with their mid-life crises by spending two weeks herding cattle at a dude ranch. Their guide out on the range, Curly (played by Jack Palance), possessed many Wild Man traits. Though at his core he was a gentle man with purpose, he was also rugged, close to the earth, and at times fierce. People knew he wasn't to be messed with. And yet his fierceness did not turn to wanton violence.

Curly showed yet another association with the Wild Man during his time alone with Mitch (Billy Crystal). He took Mitch under his wing, taught him a few skills, and gave him some profound advice for living. Curly served as Mitch's mentor for a brief time, helping him in a way his father never could have. Iron John, the Wild Man of the fairy tale, also served as the boy's mentor, advising and guiding him in the wisest directions. The mentor and the Wild Man are related because both stand outside the "normal" channels we pass through as we grow up. They challenge us to go beyond what is expected or assumed of us and trust our deepest urges and instincts about ourselves.

A final, vital characteristic of the Wild Man is his connection to the earth. Iron John was first discovered at the bottom of a bog, and later, when he was set free, he lived in the forest. Something about his character and his wisdom came from the earth itself. By honoring and respecting the earth, I honor the Wild Man within me; and by honoring my own Wild Man energy, I am drawn to care more about the earth. My attitude toward nature both reflects and informs the events of my inner self.

Let me give an example. For most of my life I have avoided water, as in rain, swimming pools, the ocean, or deep water. And I've never been a good swimmer. I didn't want to take swimming lessons as a young child—or was embarrassed to—so I grew fearful and ashamed about swimming early on. As I grew older, I shoved down my shame and told people that I wasn't much of a water person.

Then, more recently, my journey inward began. I started to explore my soul, searching its depths for the many undiscovered parts of myself, things that affected my life every day but somehow eluded my awareness. I did this exploring by means of therapy, reading, journaling, keeping track of my dreams, attending the men's support group, and taking time to be quiet and listen to my inner feelings. Along the way it occurred to me that going down into my soul was a lot like diving into the ocean. The archetype of water as soul-stuff has been around for centuries, but I was only beginning to get in touch with that archetype in myself. Without making a conscious decision about it, I found myself more drawn to water and less afraid of it.

My wife, Nancy, played a big part in this, as she has loved the ocean from her earliest days, and has spent nearly every summer of her life at the Jersey shore. When we visited her mother's beach house there, I watched Nance long for the ocean each day, how she listened to it, gazed at it, touched it, and immersed herself in it. She ate and drank of it as if it were her sacrament. Though I appreciated her spirit and secretly coveted it, all I could do at first was keep the ocean at a distance. I loved to look at it, but I didn't want to get too close. And I didn't like getting sand all over me either.

But as time passed and my inner journey continued, a thought struck me: I had been approaching my inner world in the same manner that I had been approaching the sea. I felt embarrassed and afraid to go inward. I appreciated with my head the beauty of my soul, but I remained detached from it, only dabbling around its edges where I wouldn't get too dirty. Not until I allowed myself to jump in, to dive and float and move about in the waters of my soul would I truly feel its depth and expanse and awesomeness.

And so as I took the leap into the deep currents of my soul, I felt drawn to the ocean's depths as well. Nature was actually working with me in my own growth, not only as a mirror but as a guide. That realization brought a sense of peace and oneness with the earth, a feeling that I was on the right track with my life. It helped to give me a clearer sense of who I am. Though I'm still not a good swimmer, I now feel a new kinship with the ocean.

North American culture has led us increasingly to distance ourselves from nature, to live in spite of it rather than in harmony with it. We treat nature as something to insulate ourselves from or something to manipulate to fit our own purposes. Unfortunately, the more we close ourselves off from nature, the more we tend to abuse or neglect it, which is precisely what we've done this century. We haven't just ignored the Wild Man, we've murdered him.

Passive men, I believe, must bear a major part of the responsibility for the current poor health of our planet. So much of the earth's pollution has resulted from naive, thoughtless, or downright greedy decisions made by corporate CEOs, most of whom are men. Today, some corporations appear to be looking more closely at the effects of their business activity on the environment. My impression, however, is that the motive for whatever changes have taken place has more to do with profits rather than prophets. Right now it's popular to be environmentally minded, and it might just improve business if the company devises a clever media campaign.

Of course it's not just "they," the Big Corporations, that have fouled this world's air, water, and soil. It's all of us. We work for those corporations, we buy their stock, we use their products, and we watch the (often excellent) PBS specials they sponsor. Even if we boycott those companies, we still contribute to the environmental malaise in other ways—by driving cars, wasting water, spraying chemicals on our lawns, and so on. Some of it is an unavoidable part of twentieth-century American living, but much of it is not. The sooner we admit—everyone, but especially men—that we have been a large part of the problem, the sooner we'll be able to grieve over what we've done to our world and take steps to reverse the decline.

But true change won't occur merely by saving our soda cans or reusing our grocery store bags. Something more fundamental needs to happen, down in our souls. We men need to listen to the cries of the Wild Man within us. We need to reestablish our relationship to the earth, not as a commodity to be avoided or manipulated, but as a living part of our being. We need to accept that we are a part of nature and nature is a part of us. Strange as it may sound, the more kinship we feel with the earth, the clearer our sense of identity becomes. Things come into perspective.

We see not only that we humans are the "highest" created beings, but that with the power God has given us over nature also comes the greatest amount of responsibility for its care and preservation. We must not misinterpret God's command to "subdue the earth." If we stand back in awe at the vast grandeur and beauty of creation, we will gain a clearer view of our smallness and powerlessness before God. Yes, we are created in his image, but we are *created*. In the final analysis, we are merely participating in nature, not directing it. We see our place in the order of things, and remember that we serve a Creator.

In the book of Genesis, one of the first tasks God gave to people was to rule responsibly over his creation, to watch over the earth's plants and animals. "The Lord God took the man and put him in the Garden of Eden to work it and take care of it" (2:15). Jesus lived his short life close to the earth, working with wood as a carpenter, commanding the wind and the waves to be still, using nature's images and cycles in his teaching to capture the essence of the Kingdom of God.

As I learn to identify the parts of this world that have been abused and neglected, I can do the same for parts of my self that I've ignored or mistreated. To be passive is to say that others should take care of the environment, and that others should fix our inner problems. The Wild Man can give us the fierceness and the resolve to take personal responsibility for both.

THE WARRIOR WITHIN

At first, passive men may react to the idea of awakening the inner Warrior by saying, "Hey wait—I don't want to become a terrorist!" Thankfully, this is not what the Warrior is all about. When a man is aggressive in his approach to life, persistent, decisive, disciplined, and aware of his boundaries, he possesses a strong inner Warrior. My own Warrior must have been killed off before third grade, when I began piano lessons. I thought I wanted to learn to play, but I could not bring myself to practice. I just wanted to be able to sit down at the keys and produce great music. Perhaps I didn't want to learn badly enough. But I suspect that I had already lost touch with the part of me that could make my body practice.

In ninth grade, I first realized that something like a Warrior was missing in me. I played second string on the junior varsity football team and spent most of my time on the bench. One reason was that the first-string guy, Gary, stood four inches taller and thirty pounds heavier than I. The other reason took me a while to figure out. At times I felt frustrated that the coach kept playing Gary, because he made a lot of mistakes on the field. Whenever I played, which wasn't much, I rarely if ever made a mistake. So I started watching Gary more closely during each game. What was it about him, other than size, that made him first string?

Sometime in mid-season the awareness dawned on me: What Gary had that I didn't was the ability to throw his entire self (literally) into the football game, to play with everything he had. Yes, he made mistakes, but he also made things happen on the field—completed passes and big blocks on offense, and crunching tackles and forced fumbles on defense. I didn't know what the rest of his life was like, but when it came to football, Gary gave it his all. I, on the other hand, knew that some part of me was holding back whenever I ran onto the field. My head helped me to avoid doing the wrong thing, but somehow my feet and my body never got into the action. I felt less like a player and more like an observer, lingering on the fringes of each play, wondering how I looked. I made very few errors, but I never scored touchdowns or made any big plays either. Whether I needed to let go of some fear or kick myself in the butt, I wasn't sure.

Many men with a weak inner Warrior have the same

feeling about the tasks and responsibilities of life. We know something is required of us, but we don't have the resources to charge into the fray and make things happen. Something in us is missing. At one point in the Iron John tale, the boy wants to defend in battle the king he is serving, but all he has is a three-legged horse. That missing fourth leg represents the part of us that has been wounded, shamed, or killed off by hostile intruders during childhood. Yet we passive men desperately need that leg if we are to rise to the challenges of adult manhood.

One way we can resurrect the inner Warrior is to learn from the warriors of the ancient myths and stories, who embodied a variety of traits. The first of these is aggressiveness, which is not hostility but rather a seize-the-day attitude toward life. Warriors don't wait around to see what happens; instead, they make the first move, sometimes to defend, sometimes to attack, sometimes to improve their position. Even when they are not engaged in battle, they maintain a posture of active watchfulness. Translated into twentieth-century life, the inner Warrior enables a man to take the initiative in attacking his tasks and problems before they overwhelm him. He is able to anticipate, plan, and prepare for situations ahead of time. Once he starts something—a project, a diet, a job, a relationship—he doesn't give up, but sticks with it, following through to its completion, regardless of the sacrifice that is required.

A second Warrior trait is awareness and firm protection of boundaries. Mythological warriors were often sent to defend the borders of the kingdom from invaders. A man's inner Warrior enables him to keep his personal boundaries intact. This does not mean closing everyone out, but rather alerting the man to whoever or whatever may be trying to enter—a person, an opinion or judgment, a temptation— and then enforcing the man's choice to allow or not to allow it in.

Passive men struggle with boundary issues in a big way. It's so hard for us to tell just where we end and another person begins. Very likely our boundaries were broken down when we were children. Perhaps a rageful father blasted them to pieces with verbal or physical abuse, leaving us defenseless. Or possibly an overinvolved mother enticed us into unlocking our gates and giving her the key, thus allowing other women to charm us easily as we grew older. In one case the Warriors are "killed," and in the other they are put under a trance, but either way, our boundaries have been undermined. When this happens, we find it extremely difficult to draw a line between our needs and someone else's, between our opinions and theirs, even between our own feelings and theirs. Then everything gets muddled, and we lose touch with our own individual, separate self. Who we are depends on how the person closest to us is feeling. Another way of saying it is that we become codependent.

For most of my first marriage, I figured that if my wife was sad, then I should be sad too, and if she was happy, only then was it okay for me to be happy. I had so little sense of my own self that I allowed her feelings to come in and take over. If I had had a stronger Warrior, I could have kept those boundaries distinct. I can acknowledge her feelings, I can talk with her about her feelings, and I can even help her do something about her feelings, but the Warrior keeps me ever mindful that they are *her* feelings and not necessarily mine. They do not have to invade my psyche and take control of who I am. She has every right to those feelings, but I also have the right to recognize and express my own, whether they are the same or different.

In general, I've found that the boundary line between passive men and the women they interact with is extremely thin and sometimes nonexistent. I've seen it happen again and again in groups where both men and women were present: A passive man will be somewhat stiff and superficial when he meets another man, but shortly thereafter I'll notice how relaxed and warm and animated he gets with that man's wife or with some other woman in the room. He often (though not always) has no illicit intentions about this woman; he simply finds it easier to share his feelings with her than with other men.

I know this not only from observation, but because I have done it myself. Nancy and I would return from a party or gathering, and as we compared notes about interesting people we met, I would inevitably talk about the women. When she called attention to my pattern, I balked at first, but then realized she had a point. Over the course of my life, I could think of many women I had been close friends with, but only a handful of men. I've always been drawn to reveal more of myself to women, and to invite them to reveal themselves to me. Somehow my defenses seemed to drop more quickly with women; I was hooked into them more easily. On the other hand, I kept up my guard with men, revealing little of myself, remaining a little suspicious. It occurred to me that this pattern paralleled the kind of relationships I had with my parents: I was extremely close and vulnerable with my mother, and standoffish with my father. Now I was seeing that these parental influences were resulting in too rigid boundaries between me and men, and too "soft" boundaries between me and women. There was an imbalance that needed to be corrected.

But what's wrong with a man sharing his feelings with a woman? Why should he have to stop? It's not really a matter of stopping as much as becoming aware of boundaries and learning when (or if) it is appropriate to cross them. Here is where the Warrior can serve us, by alerting us when a boundary is about to be crossed—by us or by someone else. The Warrior helps us to be attentive, to make conscious choices. He may alert us in certain situations with feelings such as danger, confusion, or a sense of "losing oneself," in order to prompt us to look more closely at what is happening to our boundaries. He may send us messages from within such as, "Whoa—you're telling this woman things you've never even said to your wife," or "Hey, you might be undermining the trust between you and your wife by spending so much time alone with this woman," or "Attention, this is only your second date with this woman and you're about to get in bed with her!" We honor the Warrior part of ourselves when we stop and listen to these messages, reflect on them, and then make active choices. This will not always be easy, because boundary issues can vary from person to person. But as passive men learn the voice of their Warrior, they will be more discerning in their relationships (with both women and men) and less likely to trust others too quickly. They will feel more solid and crisp in their sense of self. And they will be able to follow through with firmness in taking action to keep boundaries clear.

Another Warrior characteristic is the ability to carry on a fair and clean fight. Warriors don't fight all the time, but when they do, they do it skillfully, adhering to the established forms and rules, and using the proper equipment. In the martial arts, form and discipline are of the utmost importance; fighting is viewed as art, not brutality. As recently as three hundred years ago, European warfare was highly ritualized. What does this mean for a man's inner Warrior? For one thing, he views interpersonal conflict as having less to do with winning than with growth. The Warrior realizes that conflict is not necessarily a bad thing, something to be avoided. He knows that a good fight between him and his wife, for instance, can clarify issues and lead to greater understanding.

But a good fight doesn't come easily; it requires practice and discipline from both parties. It means laying down ground rules in advance that both sides agree to follow. To fight fairly, a man needs to be aware of his full self—his emotions, his body, and his desires, as well as his mind. From this fuller awareness he arrives at a stance, which he expresses forthrightly, not as a rigid, absolute position, but as a way of clearly showing his viewpoint. The Warrior enables him not only to be clear and direct, but to stay on his own side of the boundary between him and his partner: He is able to say, "I need . . . ," "I feel . . . ," "I want . . . ," rather than the judging, finger-pointing "You . . . you . . . you."

He also listens actively to the other side, giving her the same freedom to express herself. Because a Warrior has prepared for battle by bringing his armor and his weapons with him, he can take it when he is hit by an arrow; he doesn't roll over and die, like so many passive men do in arguments with their wives. Instead, he maintains his stance, continues the give-and-take, and uses his ingenuity to make concessions but also ask for them from his wife. He has the strength and discipline to stick with the conflict until some kind of resolution is reached.

The Warrior in a man needs a certain amount of self-control to be effective. He needs to be aware of his feelings and express them, but he cannot allow feelings alone to dictate his actions. If he does, rage or violence or judgment can take over. The *Star Wars* film epic illustrates what can happen without self-control. In the climactic duel between Jedi Knight Luke Skywalker and Darth Vader, Luke discovers that when he gives in to his anger, he can feel himself being won over by the "dark side of the Force." The true Warrior learns to be angry but not rageful, firm but not rigid, straightforward but not judgmental, asking for but not demanding, compromising but not selling out.

Still another vital trait of the Warrior is derived from one of his weapons, the sword. We usually think of a sword as something people kill with, but mythologically, the sword's role is to cut apart, to divide, to separate things that shouldn't be joined. When a man's inner Warrior uses his sword in this way, he will be decisive, clear-cut in his choices. In fact, the word *decide* literally means "to cut off." In light of this understanding of swords, the meaning of Jesus' cryptic statement in Matthew 10:34—"I did not come to bring peace, but a sword"—becomes more clear. Similarly, the apostle Paul, in his description of the "armor" a Christian should wear, speaks of the "sword of the Spirit, which is the Word of God" (Ephesians 6:17). And the author of Hebrews describes the Bible as "sharper than any double-edged sword" (4:12). The image is appropriate, because the words of Jesus and the Bible cut to the core of who we are, separating the self we project to the world and the self we know we are on the inside. If we take him and his words seriously, then we will not always be at peace— with ourselves or with others. At times we will have to cut ourselves off from an unhealthy relationship, a destructive pattern of behavior, a temptation, an addiction, an outmoded way of viewing the world. This is a painful but necessary part of standing up for what we believe. But just as a tree that has been pruned grows fuller and healthier, we also will grow stronger in our identity as we prune the things in life that cause us to compromise our true selves.

In short, the Warrior's sword makes it possible for us to make distinctions, to choose one thing and not another. His approach stands in stark contrast to that of passive men, who have lost or forgotten their swords. Some choose too many things at once, making it impossible to pursue any of the choices with much passion. Others don't know what they want, or are afraid to offend someone by going for what they want, and end up doing nothing.

I very much identify with this aspect of passivity, since I came out of a family and a religious subculture in which pleasing others and serving others was supposed to be a person's top priority. Neither is bad if kept in balance with one's own needs and desires, but I had lost my balance early on, and lived primarily for other people. I chose to do everything that helped others or brought me the approval or praise of others, including (I thought) the approval of God. I joined church committees, taught Sunday school, led the youth group, sang in the choir, and I had to go out practically every evening. I simply couldn't say no. As a result, I didn't carry out any of my commitments particularly well, I didn't enjoy them as much, and I burned myself out. I left no time for my own growth. Had I wielded my Warrior sword, I could have chosen one kind of service I wanted to render, given my full self to it, and still could have been able to care for the needs of my own soul.

Choosing the "one thing" applies not only to a church commitment or a weekend activity, but also to the major choices of life such as marriage and vocation. Getting married is saying yes to one woman and no to all others. Choosing a vocation (as opposed to a job, or even a career) is finding the one thing that ignites one's desire more than anything else. Both of these choices challenge a man to listen to his innermost voices, his deepest desires, and determine what (or who) it is that he really loves. And having identified that "one thing," he employs the inner Warrior to help him pursue it with every fiber of his being, and endure whatever hardship or sacrifice his pursuit may entail.

The final trait of a true Warrior is his loyalty to the King. In spite of all his power, strength, and decisiveness, the Warrior never acts on his own authority. He always follows the orders of his King. So for a man to awaken the Warrior within, he must also discover the inner King for him to serve.

THE TRANSCENDENT KING

As passive men, we tend to be unaware of the deeper parts of ourselves. Instead, we think that our outer layers comprise all, or nearly all, of our total self. The outermost layer is the mask we put on for relating to the world. It has many valuable and necessary functions for everyday life, but is far from being our full personality. The next layer includes the things we consciously know about ourselves but rarely or never show in public; only our wife or a close friend may know about them. Perhaps the next layer includes a handful of fears or longings that we've never shared with anyone. I mentioned earlier that all of these conscious parts of ourselves add up to—if we're lucky—only five percent of our total self. Beneath these layers, we hit the trap door to our unconscious, the dark void in which the deepest, truest aspects of our being lay hidden.

We've been exploring some of that uncharted territory in the past few chapters, and perhaps we've introduced ourselves to the Wild Man and the Warrior archetypes (among others) who live down there. But if we keep journeying downward, we'll eventually reach the center, the core of our self. Here we can discover a man's most important archetype, the King. Through this King we come as close as is humanly possible to knowing who we are. Through him we also come to know God.

The foremost trait of the mythological King is his connection to transcendence. The King's power and authority rest not in himself, but are derived from God. As long as the King remains in a receptive relationship with God, his kingdom will prosper, law and order will prevail, and the people will be blessed. If he denies the divine source of his authority or tries to claim it for himself, chaos will ensue in his kingdom.

At the personal level, the inner King brings order and purpose into a man's life. He knows the "one thing" that is most important to the man, shows him how to order his life around it, and helps him use wisely whatever resources are available. He also connects that "one thing" to a transcendent cause or purpose. Put another way, the King shows us how our deepest desire fits into our life story and how it fits into the great Story. He gives us a clearer picture of where our life is going, and where it needs to go.

Unfortunately, many men, especially passive men, have been unable to access (or even find) this King within them. As a result, we have felt aimless, purposeless, directionless. Robert Bly explains why in the *Iron John* chapter entitled "The Hunger for the King in a Time with No Father." He says that King energy flows downward, from the Sacred or Divine King through actual flesh-and-blood kings or rulers and finally through the father. In other words, a boy looks first to his father for a glimpse of what the King is like, and then to earthly "kings" or leaders. Between these two, the theory goes, he will learn to recognize the King in himself, and partake of the order and blessing that is available from the Divine King. But in today's world, so many of us men have had fathers who weren't there for us, and so our first link to the King is missing or damaged. Then, as we look for earthly kings who can serve as models, we find that no living king carries the divine radiance of a King Solomon, King Arthur, or a King Charlemagne. Neither has any political leader of recent history, although some have felt John F. Kennedy had a regal aura about him. There goes the second link.

When we can't find our own inner King or don't bother to look for him or don't believe we even have one, something interesting happens: we tend to let others be our King—our wives, our bosses, business gurus, ministers, sports figures, rock or movie stars. Once again we are faced with our passivity—looking outside of ourselves rather than inside. By allowing these people to plan our schedules, make our decisions for us, and tell us what to believe, how to talk and what to wear, we think that our inner lives will somehow fall into place. The plan may seem to work for a while, but inevitably these people are unable to "carry our King" for us, and the relationship breaks down. Our wives grow disgruntled because we have no drive or conviction that is our own, and they don't want to be in charge of our lives. Bosses grow weary of employees who merely do what they're told and never take initiative.

In Christian circles, I've seen many men base their decision about which church to attend entirely on the minister and his sermons, as if all the characteristics of a perfect church were bound up in a weekly homily. Then, after choosing the church with the "right" minister, they weigh every word of his messages, week after week. If he says anything that makes them feel too uncomfortable, poof. They're out the door, looking for a new church. Unquestionably a congregation's minister or priest is important, but there is so much more to a church (and the Church) than the minister. Further, if too many people project their need for a King onto the minister, trouble may be just around the corner—for the people and for the minister. The pressure of so many people's expectations could cause the minister to think he has all the answers, to have an affair, or to get caught up in shady financial deals. Or he may stay clean but decide to move on to another congregation. In either case, the church falls apart, at least until its members can find someone else to project their King on.

With no effective models of King energy in the world, how can men ever find the King in themselves or establish a relationship to the Divine King? I'm still struggling to answer that question in a specific way for myself. I have so desperately wanted to feel that my life was headed in a purposeful, redemptive, fulfilling direction. I've wanted to experience the presence of that King in me, as well as the ongoing presence of God, the Divine King. Others I've spoken to have expressed the same hunger. At a men's gathering I attended one weekend, a man stood up and confessed how badly he wanted to get in touch with his inner King. As I watched him speak, I was struck by his appearance: He had dark, shoulder-length hair, a beard, and penetrating eyes. My immediate first impression was that he looked like Jesus, the King of Kings for the Christian. Perhaps it was his unconscious way of striving to connect with the King in himself.

I believe I have spent much of my life trying to find my King by going up rather than down. I figured (unconsciously) that I could jump over my father and over the older men and leaders who might be role models, and land right in the arms of God. In high school I ran for president (or Top Dog) of every organization I could—student council, Key Club, school paper—thinking that would awaken the ordering, purposeful part of myself. It didn't, but I kept on jumping higher, to the spiritual level. I attended a Christian college and majored in biblical studies, thinking that if I gained lots of spiritual knowledge, that I'd become a spiritual person. Or that four years of heady information about God would automatically create a relationship with God. That didn't really happen either.

Instead, I felt a yawning chasm between me and God. I believed in his existence, his goodness, and his care for me, but I felt so distant, so disconnected from him. And I had little of his power and energy in my life. Not until recently did I begin to realize that no matter how hard I try, I cannot jump across that gap and reach God directly. To find him, I must follow a certain path, the road that leads downward and inward. It seems that the further down I go into myself, and the better I get to know who I really am, the closer I am to reaching my inner King, and therefore God.

Finding myself, finding my King, and finding God are

not the same thing, but they're closely related. The Bible says we are created in the "image" and "likeness" of God (Genesis 1:26), which I take to mean that God has put something of himself in every human being. In men, the masculine side of God's image predominates; in women, the feminine side. Frederick Buechner calls this image of God our "original self," and describes it as follows:

> Those original selves which we were born with and which I believe we continue in some measure to be . . . still echo with the holiness of their origin. I believe that what Genesis suggests is that this original self, with the print of God's thumb still upon it, is the most essential part of who we are and is buried deep in all of us as a source of wisdom and strength and healing which we can draw upon or, with our terrible freedom, not draw upon as we choose.[2]

Wisdom, strength, and healing—these are all characteristics of the true King. When we encounter this inner King, the only proper thing to do is to submit to him, freely and joyfully. Actually, there need to be several layers of submission in a man. His outer, conscious self submits to the deeper wisdom and direction of his inner King, and the inner King submits to the Divine King, God. This is the process that is encouraged by support groups which use the Twelve Steps of Alcoholics Anonymous (and its variations). Once the participants admit that their addictions or compulsions have rendered their lives "unmanageable," and believe that only a Power greater than themselves can bring stability back into their lives, they "made a decision to turn our will and our lives over the care of God as we understood Him" (Step 3). In a very real sense, these people are submitting to their inner King. That submission has led to a reordering of their priorities, and a clearer sense of direction.

The inward journey we take in search of our King will be long and sometimes difficult, though not without its rewards. In fact, it is impossible to find the King on our own. Therapy, meditation, reading, and journaling will help, but ultimately we can find the King only with the aid of the King himself. Fortunately, the King refuses to hibernate in his castle all the time; he likes to travel around the kingdom and visit his people. So, as we move toward our inner King, let us not forget that he wants to make himself known to us too. He wants to bring order and purpose into our lives. Perhaps our role is not so much to chase after him, but to be ready for him, to prepare our souls for him when he appears. Jesus describes himself as knocking on the door of our souls, waiting for us to open it. If we do, he says he'll come in and dine with us (Revelation 3:20).

Participating in a Christian church service can be one way of drawing closer to our inner King and the Divine King. Some churches may require a lot more of our imagination than others, but in general going to church can be viewed as having an audience with Christ the King. Often the sanctuary resembles a king's chamber, and the orderly progression of the service (especially in liturgical churches such as Roman Catholic and Episcopal) parallels the ceremony and protocol one would encounter in a visit with a human king. We are encouraged to honor and worship the King, listen to his sacred decrees, and receive his blessings. We even share an intimate meal with the King by eating bread and drinking wine in the ritual known as the Eucharist or Holy Communion. All of these external actions are designed to awaken us and remind us of an inner reality, the presence of Christ the King within us. Yes, it's possible to rattle off the responses and go through the motions without feeling their power, but not if we truly want to commune with the King. If we prepare ourselves beforehand, and think of church less as a concert or a lecture and more as a drama in which every person plays a part, I believe we can experience our King's presence and power.

The King not only brings order into our lives, but also

blessing. To be blessed is to be supremely valued, affirmed, and validated—something that men desperately need these days. So few of us have received adequate praise from our fathers or even the validation of a mentor. When a man receives a divine blessing through his inner King, the effect can be tremendously empowering, as in this song by Bruce Cockburn:

> *When you've got a dream like mine*
> *Nobody can take you down*
> *When you've got a dream like mine*
> *Nobody can push you around . . .*
>
> *When you know even for a moment*
> *That it's your time*
> *Then you can walk with the power*
> *Of a thousand generations*[3]

Finally, the order and blessing of the King lead to a fruitful, productive life, one that is creative, fulfilling, and makes a difference in the world or our part of it. Maybe this fruitfulness will come as our life takes a new direction, or perhaps it will occur in our present situation. Regardless of what we are doing, when we are connected with the King, we feel more alive, more sure of who we are, and more in touch with God.

Wild Man, Warrior, and King—three inner characters that can transform a passive man into an active, passionate, life-giving man. We need to grieve the loss of these archetypes in our childhood, and we need to grieve their disappearance from the psychic landscape of today's Western culture. But in the absence of contemporary role models—mortal or mythological—we need to focus on our own inner work of resurrecting these parts of ourselves.

The most important thing to remember is that these archetypes, and many others, are present in every man. All of the resources for changing our life, including the divine resource of God himself, lie within us. If we are willing to search our inner depths for these buried parts of ourselves and carry them up into our everyday, conscious life, we will begin to see our masculine identity grow stronger and crisper.

THE SUPREME MODEL FOR MEN

As a Christian in the men's movement, I cannot help but call attention to the role Jesus Christ can play in helping men to reclaim their masculinity. Not the weak, effeminate Christ portrayed in many children's stories, Sunday school materials, and films, but rather the Christ of the Bible, who comes across as a much deeper, more multidimensional, more balanced man. It is important to keep this biblical Christ separate from the plastic, toned-down Jesus fabricated by our culture and by the institutional church. When I look at the biblical Jesus Christ, I have been struck again and again by the parallels between his character and that of the mature man as set forth by the men's movement.

For one thing, Jesus embodied all three of the archetypes discussed above. His connection to the Wild Man is evident in his baptism by John, a prophet who lived in the wilderness and ate locusts and wild honey. Jesus showed fierceness in driving the moneylenders from the Temple and in many of his encounters with the Pharisees. From the nature imagery in his teaching to his command over the wind and the waves, he demonstrated his closeness to the earth. The Warrior is seen in Jesus' ability to resist temptation, maintain a disciplined life, and follow through in doing the will of his Father, even though he knew he would have to suffer. He also displayed the Warrior's cunning, discernment, firmness, and clarity in his dialogues with skeptics. As for the King, Jesus embodied this archetype as no man has ever done. His divine authority, power, and energy were immediately recognized by those around him. He performed miracles, healed the sick, blessed people, forgave sins, made new laws, and reinterpreted old ones. His presence and his teaching brought order to the lives of those who followed him. Though his life was short, he lived every minute of it with purpose and passion. It's no wonder that the account of his adult life, death, and resurrection is often called the Passion. His life moved unswervingly toward the "one thing" he was put on earth to do: endure the cross and overcome death in order to achieve redemption for the world.

Beyond these archetypal connections, Jesus also modeled the steps and stages a man must go through to reach maturity. He effectively bonded with and separated from both of his parents, working alongside his father as a carpenter before his father's (probable) death, and maintaining a good relationship with his mother yet not allowing her to interfere with his central purpose. The only recorded event of Jesus' childhood—when he left his parents and spent three days in the temple talking with the elders—has strong initiatory overtones. As he grew older, he moved comfortably into the world of men by assembling a close-knit group of twelve male disciples. He not only instructed these men, but also shared his feelings with them, especially in his final days when he needed their support. While Jesus did not appear to have an earthly mentor, he clearly saw its value and devoted a major part of his ministry to the mentoring of his disciples.

Jesus did not skip over the inner work of facing his fears, his dark feelings, and his temptations. He often went away by himself to pray. He is described as "a man of sorrows, acquainted with grief." He knew the importance of descent and "ashes work." The Bible says that he "humbled himself," "made himself nothing, taking the very nature of a servant." He knew the value of suffering in building character. Because he had a keen awareness that he would die, he lived intensely and purposefully, and as he died, he was able to say, "It is finished."

Christ also made frequent use of myth and symbol in his teaching. He often appealed to Old Testament stories, which were part of the Jewish mythology of that day. But he took them a step further and claimed that he was the continuation, the fulfillment of those stories. He used parables, a close relative of myths, as a teaching tool to reach his listeners. He also employed symbolic images such as water, wind, bread, and light to describe how a person relates to God. He showed a respect for ritual in his baptism, in some of his healing practices, and in his officiating at the Last Supper. And finally, he showed an understanding of his life as a story, while also seeing how his life story fit into God's great Story of the creation and salvation of the world. This brief overview of Jesus hardly scratches the surface, but I hope it provides a starting point for passive men who are looking for mature masculine role models. I would also urge Christian passive men to examine the image of Jesus they are carrying within them. Might it be time to take a fresh look?

In this book, I've tried to share some of the discoveries I've made so far in my journey from passivity to conscious living. Even after several years of self-exploration, I feel as though I've just begun. And yet I can see that my life has changed in many ways for the better. I know more clearly now what being a man is all about, and I'm chipping away at the buried fragments of my male identity so as to make them an active part of my everyday life. When I do my work, relate to Nancy and Brendan, and interact with the outside world, I feel there's a lot more of myself involved. I'm living less from the outside in and more from the inside out. I feel more real.

Resolving one's father relationship, learning to relate to other men, exploring the dark and hidden parts of oneself, awakening the fuller self through myth, viewing one's life as a story, rousing the inner Wild Man and Warrior, choosing the "one thing"—all of these will serve to break our bondage to passivity. They will also bring us closer and closer to our masculine center, where the King awaits us, and behind him, God himself.

Notes

INTRODUCTION

1. Thanks to Robert Bly for the "rattle" image, which he uses in *A Little Book on the Human Shadow,* ed. by William Booth (San Francisco: HarperSan-Francisco, 1988), 31.

CHAPTER 1

1. Robert Bly, *Iron John: A Book About Men* (Reading, Massachusetts: Addison-Wesley, 1990), 2–3.
2. M. Scott Peck, *The Road Less Traveled* (New York: Touchstone/Simon and Schuster, 1978), 17.

CHAPTER 2

1. Chang Tsi, quoted by Werner Heisberg in *Symbolism in Religion and Literature,* ed. by Rollo May (New York: George Braziller, Inc., 1960), 225.
2. C. G. Jung, *The Portable Jung,* edited by Joseph Campbell (New York: Penguin, 1976), 466.
3. Andrew Kimbrell, "A Time for Men to Pull Together," *Utne Reader* (May/June 1991).
4. "Cat's in the Cradle" by Harry Chapin and Sandy Chapin © 1974 Story Songs, Ltd. Used by permission.
5. Bly, *Iron John,* 96.
6. Robert A. Johnson, *HE: Understanding Masculine Psychology* (King of Prussia, Pa.: Religious Publishing Co., 1974; Harper Perennial Library edition, 1977), 50.
7. Jung, *The Portable Jung,* 148–149.
8. *Ibid.,* 147.

CHAPTER 3

Epigraph: "All This Time," words and music by Sting © 1990 Magnetic Publishing, Ltd./Blue Turtle Music. Used by permission. All rights reserved.
1. Ric Williams, "This Must Be the Place: An Annotated, Nonlinear Meditative History of the Men's Movement," *MAN!* (Fall, 1991), 15. I am grateful to Mr. Williams for the general approach I've taken in giving background on the men's movement.
2. *Esquire,* for example, could never have done a serious treatment of the men's movement (see the Oct. 1991 issue) because it would be a direct insult to its rich and powerful advertisers, who want men to maintain their materialistic, image- and status-oriented approach to life.
3. Patrick M. Arnold, S.J., "In Search of the Hero: Masculine Spirituality and Liberal Christianity," *America* (October 7, 1989). Before his death, Arnold

released the book *Wildmen, Warriors and Kings: Masculine Spirituality and the Bible* (New York: Crossroad, 1991), an insightful look at men's issues from a theologically liberal Christian perspective.

4. Bly, *Iron John*, 2–4.

5. Melody Beattie, *Codependent No More* (San Francisco: Harper/Hazelden, 1987), 31.

6. I do not intend to convey that the absent-or-abusive-father/overcompensating-mother pattern described here is in itself the total picture of what makes a dysfunctional family; many factors come into play. But this pattern occurs frequently in dysfunctional families, especially in those of boys who grew up to become passive men.

7. Barrie Peterson of Mahwah, N.J., has compiled these branches of men's activity into a "Men's Movements Tree." Even a casual look at this tree reveals the incredible diversity—political, psychological, mythopoetic, and spiritual—among men's groups. The diagram also gives a sense of perspective: Wildman gatherings, for instance, are a mere twig. For a copy of the "Men's Movements Tree," write to Barrie Peterson at Resources for Men Northeast, 7 Chestnut Street, Mahwah, NJ 07430.

8. Sam Keen, *Fire in the Belly: On Being a Man* (New York: Bantam Books, 1991), 65. Copyright 1991 Sam Keen. Used by permission of Bantam Books, a division of Bantam/Doubleday/Dell Publishing Group, Inc.

9. Jill Johnston, "Why Iron John Is No Gift to Women," *The New York Times Book Review* (February 23, 1992).

10. Bly, *Iron John*, x.

11. "Women on Men: The Uneasy State of Masculinity Now," *Esquire* (October 1991).

12. Deborah Tannen, *You Just Don't Understand: Women and Men in Conversation* (New York: Ballantine Books, 1991), 17.

CHAPTER 4

Epigraph: Loudon Wainwright III, "A Father and a Son." Copyright © 1992 Snowden Music, Inc. All rights reserved. Used by permission.

1. Johnson, *HE*, 28–29.

2. Bly, *Iron John*, 42.

3. James Hillman articulated these distinctions between one's father and a mentor at a men's conference in New York City, November 2–3, 1991.

4. Rainer Maria Rilke, *Letters to a Young Poet*, translation by M. D. Herter Norton, revised edition (New York: W. W. Norton & Co., 1954), 52–53.

5. A few evangelical parachurch organizations (usually oriented to youth) such as InterVarsity Christian Fellowship and The Navigators have emphasized the importance of mentors in building one's faith. Often they call it "discipleship." They suggest that a person will grow spiritually as he or she is "discipled" by someone older in years and/or faith (such as a staff member or graduate student), and as he or she "disciples" someone younger in the faith. The potential for abuse exists if these relationships are forced or overly authoritarian. But on the whole, they can be a valuable part of one's growth as long as they are mutually agreed upon, maintain mutual respect, stress affirmation and support, and include an honest attempt at consistent living as well as the passing on of

spiritual information. In spite of occasions when these mentor-like relationships have become unbalanced, I believe the core concept is sound.

CHAPTER 5

1. See, for example, Peck, *Road Less Traveled,* 243.

2. The parallel passage in Mark 9:36 substitutes the word *soul* for *self,* which to me implies that the self being referred to in Luke 9:25 is not the conscious self or ego, but the deeper, truer self, the self that can know and commune with God.

3. Frederick Buechner, *Telling Secrets* (San Francisco: HarperSanFrancisco, 1991), 27.

4. Keen, *Fire in the Belly,* 151.

5. See John A. Sanford, *Dreams: God's Forgotten Language* (New York: Crossroad, 1968) for an excellent treatment of dreams from a Christian perspective, including a chapter on dreams and visions in the Bible.

6. Gerald G. May, M.D., *Addiction and Grace* (San Francisco: HarperSan-Francisco, 1988), 20.

7. Keen, *Fire in the Belly,* 147.

8. Rilke, *Letters to a Young Poet,* 19–20.

9. *Ibid.,* 20–21.

10. Bruce Springsteen, "Two Faces." Copyright © 1987 by Bruce Springsteen. All rights reserved. Used by permission.

11. A good overview of the concept of the shadow is found in *A Little Book on the Human Shadow* by Robert Bly, edited by William Booth (HarperSanFrancisco, 1988), from which some of these ideas have been adapted. Another valuable introduction is *Owning Your Own Shadow: Understanding the Dark Side of the Psyche* by Robert A. Johnson (HarperSanFrancisco, 1991).

12. An interesting fact concerning the Jekyll and Hyde story: Its central images came to Stevenson in a dream. His wife suggested that he write them down as a story. From Bly, *A Little Book on the Human Shadow,* 18–19.

13. Johnson, *Owning Your Own Shadow,* 42.

CHAPTER 6

1. C. S. Lewis, preface to *George MacDonald: An Anthology* (New York: Macmillan, 1962), 21.

2. Clyde S. Kilby, "What Is Myth?" (unpublished handout from Wheaton College, Ill., English Department).

3. P. L. Travers, *What the Bee Knows: Reflections on Myth, Symbol and Story* (Wellingborough, England: The Aquarian Press, 1989), 16.

4. George MacDonald, "The Fantastic Imagination," from *A Dish of Orts* (Folcroft, Penn.: Folcroft Library Editions, 1976). Facsimile reprint of original 1882 edition.

5. C. S. Lewis, "Myth Became Fact," from *God in the Dock: Essays on Theology and Ethics* (Grand Rapids, Mich.: William B. Eerdmans, 1970), 66–67.

6. *Ibid.,* 67.

7. J. R. R. Tolkien, *The Tolkien Reader* (New York: Ballantine Books, 1966), 71–72.

8. Kilby, "What Is Myth?"

9. From J. R. R. Tolkien, *The Two Towers* (New York: Ballantine Books, 1965), II: 407–9. copyright © 1954, 1965, by J. R. R. Tolkien. Copyright © renewed 1982 by Christopher R. Tolkien, Michael H. R. Tolkien, John F. R. Tolkien, and Priscilla M. A. R. Tolkien. Reprinted by permission of Houghton Mifflin Company. All Right reserved.

I am grateful to my former English professor Joe McClatchey for his brilliant elucidation of this Tolkien passage in an undated handout entitled, " 'I wonder what sort of a tale we've fallen into?': Myth, Monomyth, and Mythopoeia in the Literature of Middle-Earth."

10. I would also credit professor Leland Ryken for reinforcing these ideas in class and in his book *Triumphs of the Imagination: Literature in Christian Perspective* (Downers Grove, Ill.: InterVarsity Press, 1979).

11. Mircea Eliade, *Myth & Reality,* translated by Willard R. Trask (New York: Harper & Row, 1963).

CHAPTER 7

Epigraph: Carol S. Pearson, *Awakening the Heroes Within: Twelve Archetypes to Help Us Find Ourselves and Transform Our World* (San Francisco: HarperSanFrancisco, 1991).

1. Robert Moore and Douglas Gillette, *King, Warrior, Magician, Lover: Rediscovering the Archetypes of the Mature Masculine* (San Francisco: HarperSanFrancisco, 1990). Moore, a Jungian analyst and scholar, was the first to explore archetypes as they related to the masculine psyche. He and Gillette are following up their first book with four more books, one for each archetype. *The King Within* and *The Warrior Within* (New York: William Morrow, 1992) are already available, and *The Magician Within* and *The Lover Within* will appear soon from the same publisher. All of Robert Moore's books and tapes on masculine psychology and spirituality can be purchased through the C. G. Jung Institute of Chicago Bookstore, 1567 Maple Avenue, Evanston, IL 60201; telephone 708-475-4848.

2. Buechner, *Telling Secrets,* 44.

3. "A Dream Like Mine" © 1991 Golden Mountain Music Corp. Words and music by Bruce Cockburn. Taken from the album *Nothing But a Burning Light.* Used by permission.

Bibliography

Arnold, Patrick M. *Wildmen, Warriors and Kings: Masculine Spirituality and the Bible*. New York: Crossroad, 1991.

Beattie, Melody. *Codependent No More: How to Stop Controlling Others and Start Caring for Yourself*. San Francisco: Harper/Hazelden, 1987.

Bly, Robert. *Iron John: A Book About Men*. Reading, Mass.: Addison-Wesley, 1990.

_____. *A Little Book on the Human Shadow*. Edited by William Booth. San Francisco: Harper & Row, 1988.

_____. *Selected Poems*. New York: Harper & Row, 1986.

_____, editor and translator. *Selected Poems of Rainer Maria Rilke*. New York: Harper & Row, 1981.

Buechner, Frederick. *Telling Secrets: A Memoir*. San Francisco: HarperSanFrancisco, 1991.

_____. *Telling the Truth: The Gospel as Tragedy, Comedy, and Fairy Tale*. San Francisco: Harper & Row, 1977.

Campbell, Joseph. *The Hero with a Thousand Faces*. Princeton: Princeton University Press/Bollingen, 1949.

_____. *Myths To Live By*. New York: Bantam, 1973.

_____, with Bill Moyers. *The Power of Myth*. New York: Doubleday, 1988.

Clift, Wallace B. *Jung and Christianity: The Challenge of Reconciliation*. New York: Crossroad, 1982.

Eliade, Mircea. *Rites and Symbols of Initiation: The Mysteries of Birth and Rebirth*. New York: Harper & Brothers, 1958, Harper Torchbooks edition 1975.

Holy Bible, New International Version. Grand Rapids: Zondervan, 1973, 1978, 1984.

Johnson, Robert A. *HE: Understanding Masculine Psychology*. New York: Harper Perennial Library, 1977.

_____. *Transformation: Understanding the Three Levels of Masculine Consciousness*. San Francisco: HarperSanFrancisco, 1991.

_____. *Owning Your Own Shadow: Understanding the Dark Side of the Psyche*. San Francisco: HarperSanFrancisco, 1991.

Jung, C. G. *The Portable Jung*. Edited by Joseph Campbell. New York: Penguin, 1976.

Keen, Sam. *Fire in the Belly: On Being a Man*. New York: Bantam, 1991.

———, and Anne Valley-Fox. *Your Mythic Journey: Finding Meaning in Your Life Through Writing and Storytelling*. Los Angeles: Jeremy P. Tarcher, 1973, 1989.

Lee, John. *The Flying Boy: Healing the Wounded Man*. Deerfield Beach, Fla.: Health Communications, 1989.

Lewis, C. S. *God in the Dock: Essays on Theology and Ethics*. Edited by Walter Hooper. Grand Rapids: Eerdmans, 1970.

May, Rollo, ed. *Symbolism in Religion and Literature*. New York: George Braziller, 1960.

May, Gerald G. *Addiction and Grace: Love and Spirituality in the Healing of Addictions*. San Francisco: HarperSanFrancisco, 1988.

Moore, Robert, and Douglas Gillette. *King, Warrior, Magician, Lover: Rediscovering the Archetypes of the Mature Masculine*. San Francisco: HarperSanFrancisco, 1990.

———. *The King Within: Accessing the King in the Male Psyche*. New York: William Morrow, 1992.

Osherson, Samuel. *Finding Our Fathers: How a Man's Life Is Shaped by His Relationship with His Father*. New York: Fawcett Columbine, 1986.

Peck, M. Scott. *The Road Less Traveled: A New Psychology of Love, Traditional Values and Spiritual Growth*. New York: Touchstone/Simon and Schuster, 1978.

Rank, Otto, Lord Raglan, and Alan Dundes. *In Quest of the Hero*. Princeton: Princeton University Press/Bollingen, 1990.

Rilke, Rainer Maria. *Letters to a Young Poet*. Translated by M. D. Herter. New York: W. W. Norton, 1954.

Sanford, John A., and George Lough. *What Men Are Like: The Psychology of Men, for Men and the Women Who Live with Them*. Mahwah, N.J.: Paulist Press, 1988.

Sanford, John A. *Dreams: God's Forgotten Language*. New York: Crossroad, 1968.

———. *The Kingdom Within: The Inner Meaning of Jesus' Sayings*. Revised edition. San Francisco: Harper & Row, 1987.

Storr, Anthony. *Solitude: A Return to the Self*. New York: Ballantine, 1988.

Tolkien, J. R. R. *The Tolkien Reader*. New York: Ballantine, 1966.

Additional Resources

While the following organizations and publications do not claim to be Christian, they do provide information on men's issues, men's groups, and workshops, books, tapes, and videos that can be useful to the discerning Christian man.

Ally Press Center, 524 Orleans Street, St. Paul, MN 55107 features "books, tapes and videos in the area of men's work, mythology and poetry, featuring Robert Bly, James Hillman, Michael Meade and Robert Moore." Write or call 1-800-729-3002 for their current catalog.

Sounds True, 735 Walnut Street, Dept. FC4, Boulder, CO 80302 publishes a general catalog of audiotapes on "myth and meaning, self-discovery, and the spiritual challenge." They also have a catalog of audiotapes exclusively on men's issues. Phone: 1-800-333-9185.

Wingspan: Journal of the Male Spirit is a quarterly sixteen-page newspaper which, since 1986, "has been representing the scope of men's work through provocative leadership interviews, workshop profiles, discussions of myth and poetry as well as timely reviews of men's book, films and tapes." It is free to anyone who asks for it (though contributions are welcomed), and currently has a circulation of 150,000. Write to *Wingspan,* Box 23550, Brightmoor Station, Detroit, MI 48223; phone 313-273-4330.

MAN!, a quarterly magazine on "Men's Issues, Relationships, and Recovery" is a thoughtful collection of interviews, reviews, and articles, as well as a useful compilations of information on men's groups and organizations around the country. A one-year subscription is $12.00 (Canada $17.00). Write to them at 1611 W. Sixth St., Austin, TX 78703, or call 512-474-6401.

For those who want to start a men's group or who want to find good material that can be used for group interaction, three books can serve as valuable resources: *A Circle of Men: The Original Manual for Men's Support Groups,* by Bill Kauth (New York: St. Martin's Press, 1992); *Tending the Fire: The Ritual Men's Group,* by Wayne Liebman (St. Paul, Minn.: Ally Press, 1991); and *Wingspan: Inside the Men's Movement,* edited by Christopher Harding (New York: St. Martin's Press, 1992). All three of these books have extensive listings of resources on groups, organizations, books, tapes, and movies dealing with men's issues.

In metropolitan areas around the country, men's centers are springing up as clearinghouses of information and resources for men. Here are a few:

On the Common Ground
250 W. 57th St., Suite 1527
New York, NY 10107
John Guarnaschelli
212-265-0584

Resources for Men Northeast
P.O. Box 137
Little Ferry, NJ 07643
Barrie Peterson
201-848-9134

Men's Council of Greater
   Washington
2114 Belvedere Blvd, #6
Silver Spring, MD 20902
Doug Giauque
301-593-8182

Men's Center of Raleigh and Wake
   County
723 West Johnson Street
P.O. Box 6155
Raleigh, NC 27628
919-832-0509

Austin Men's Center
1611 W. Sixth St.
Austin, TX 78703
512-477-9595

Earthmen Resources
P.O. Box 1034
Evanston, IL 60204

Twin Cities Men's Center
3255 Hennepin Ave. South, Suite 55
Minneapolis, MN 55408
612-822-5892

Men's Council Project
P.O. Box 17341
Boulder, CO 80301
Tom Daly
303-444-7797

Los Angeles Men's Center
9012 Burton Way
Beverly Hills, CA 90212
Stephen Johnson
213-276-9598

Seattle Men's Evolving Network
602 West Howe Street
Seattle, WA 98119
206-285-4356
or Robert Carlson 206-454-1787